Fashion Illustration

IN NEW YORK

Coordinated by Pater Sato

エディトリアル・ディレクター：赤平覚三
アート・ディレクション：タキ・オノ
デザイン：廣田武志
エディター：鮫島理子
カバーイラストレーション：アントニオ・ロペス

Fashion Illustration In New York
Copyright © 1985 Graphic-sha Publishing Co., Ltd.
1-9-12 Kudankita, Chiyoda-ku, Tokyo 102, Japan.
ISBN4-7661-0325-4

Editorial Director: Kakuzo Akahira
Art Direction/Design: Taki Ono
Design: Takeshi Hirota
Editor: Rico Samejima
Cover Illustration: Antonio Lopez

Printed in Japan

First Printing, 1985

C O N T E N T S

My Friends, My New York   **4**

Antonio Lopez アントニオ・ロペス   **8**

Jim Howard ジム・ハワード   **24**

Pedro Barrios ペドロ・バリオス   **30**

J. Crawford J. クロフォード   **36**

William Rieser ウィリアム・リーサー   **42**

David Croland デビッド・クローランド   **48**

George Stavrinos ジョージ・スタヴリノス   **54**

Kichisaburo Ogawa キチサブロー・オガワ   **60**

Michael Van Horn マイケル・ヴァン・ホーン   **62**

Martin Hoffman マーティン・ホフマン   **68**

Harvey Boyd ハービー・ボイド   **76**

Mats Gustavson マッツ・グスタブソン   **82**

Joel Resnicoff ジョエル・レズニコフ   **90**

Cathy Barancik キャシー・バランシック   **96**

Bob Hiemstra ボブ・ヒムストラ   **104**

Artists' Profile   **109**

Afterword   **126**

My Friends, My New York

I was born in Utuado, Puerto Rico, which is farm country in the Puerto Rican hills. My mother married at 14. My father was 17. It was a marriage arranged by the families. We lived there until I was 5 years old. My recollections of that time are vivid: when I first started to draw at the age of 2, my mother making clothes. I spent most of my time with her sketching dresses and making dresses from leftover fabric she would give me. Strangely enough, my father was very encouraging. When I got upset, instead of giving me a baseball bat, he'd buy me a doll. We left there when my father was drafted into the Army and moved to San Juan where I spent most of my time with my grandmother. I didn't go to school until I came to America at the age of 8. I learned to read and write from my grandparents.

I have two younger brothers. I always had a dream of coming to America. My father once showed me a postcard of Florida and told me it was New York City. It was a picture of flowers, tropical gardens, sunshine. I wanted to come to New York ever since. Finally, I arrived in New York City at night with the temperature below zero, totally unprepared and disappointed with the tall buildings and gray atmosphere of my new home in Spanish harlem, but I soon grew used to my new life.

My father worked at that time making store mannequins and it was amazing how he would actually mold plaster and paint it. I used to work with him after school putting hair on the mannequins. I was exposed to fashion through my mother, and through my father I was able to create dolls and style them. It was a wonderful time for me—my fantasies were fulfilled. In most other respects, I led a very ordinary life, playing baseball and doing things normal kids do. But I always thought my home more exciting.

In school I always would end up with the most beautiful girls, and it was because I understood them: I knew what they liked and how to please them while other boys were too busy intimidating them or teasing them. I was charming them.

My first real makeover was my mother. She blossomed around the age of 28, when she became beautiful, incredibly beautiful. She collected shoes, which I became very interested in to the point of obsession. She was the kind of woman who exuded sex. It was all learned. So I learned early that with very little you can do a lot and go a long way, and that's what I tell all my girls now.

I was brought up a Catholic, but since my father was a spiritual healer I was also influenced by white magic and its mystical aura. Around the age of 11, I decided I wanted to be a dancer, and for a year I tap danced on television children shows. But I changed my mind pretty soon after and went back to my primary interest: drawing. I was always winning contests and medals, and encouraged by all my teachers to continue my artistic career. It was in high school that my teachers suggested I do fashion illustrations since I could draw so well, and they figured I could pick up designing later. I was given the same advice at the Fashion Institute of Technology (FIT). The illustration department wanted me so they kept me there. I've always had it in the back of my mind to design clothes.

To me, the human body isn't naturally sexy. The clothes are responsible for making us aware of our sexuality, while nudity leaves little to the imagination. Clothes can serve to heighten sexuality. It's like truth when it's so obvious—there's no room for anything else. But clothes give us many choices and possibilities.

Maybe my interest in designing clothes is my attempt to do what my mother always wanted to do and was never successful at. Maybe it's my tribute to her.

So up to this point in my life, I've put my energy into fashion illustration and achieved my goals in that field. Now I have the opportunity to do fashion design, and the time to put my energy into fine arts.

The Paris Years

I met Karl Lagerfeld at his showroom in Paris while on a working trip for Elle magazine in 1969. I later moved to Paris to set up a studio, and we started socializing and quickly became close friends. Karl found us an apartment on Boulevard St. Germain which soon became the American center for wayward models and fashion celebrities of all types. Most models coming to Paris ended up there for various reasons: some out of money, some just to say hello, and some hoping to start a career. Such people as Grace Jones, Eija, Jerry Hall, Pat Cleveland, Tina Chow & Jessica Lange were a few who were always close at hand.

This was in the late 1960's when the Pop Art movement began to influence French culture. I brought this feeling to the realm of fashion illustration, and my models re-introduced hot pants and spike heels, the return of the platinum blonde, and Black beauties.

We all shared a common inspiration for exciting trends, and all had a keen eye for what would happen next. Karl became somewhat of a patron. He made certain that we and our friends Donna Jordan, Jane Forth and Corey Tippin could express our style throughout Paris and the French Riviera.

This was an exciting period in Paris, and we were largely responsible for revitalizing cafe society at La Coupole, Cafe Flore and the then unknown Club 7. This was before the word disco was invented. But we went out every night and danced until the bars closed, patronizing the Club 7 and making it what it is today. We created new dance steps to the background of American Soul music. Before we were there, the French couldn't even dance—they were still doing the Lindy. We brought over the American culture and through Karl we were able to expose it in a very influential, powerful way.

During the summers, Karl would rent a large villa in St. Tropez, and we all would go down first class (Karl would make sure to get the reservations months in advance). We would take the Tren Bleu, and fill up a baggage car with our luggage alone. This included Karl's latest fashions, custom clothes from Cerrutti, jewelry from the best shops in Paris including Lalique pieces, top hats, canes, parasols. It was a time when everyone wore makeup, had long hair, and changed their clothes at least three times a day. Perfumes like Tabac Blanc, Fracas, Jacque Fath filled the air. We rented our own Riva, had a Rolls Royce always at our disposal. Lots of toys to play with in return for our company and inspiration. In reality a deep friendship developed out of this.

We had our youth and our sensibility. One of the girls we brought over was Patti D'Arbanville. She was only 17 years old. Andy Warhol came over later and she ended up in his movies. The kind of girls we brought inspired everyone, they were so fresh and full of vitality. I once did a winged hairdo on Paloma Picasso, and a few months later, all the models were being photographed in winged hairdos. My girls usually ended up working with Guy Bourdin and Helmut Newton. In 1977 at the Yves St. Laurent collection, five of his girls were American girls I found and made into models.

We worked a lot and grew a lot. This period in our relationship ended when we got hungry for America and Karl was moving into his eighteenth century period. We both started growing in different directions. There's a closeness between us that's forever. I still feel we are somehow part of the same close family.

Since coming back to New York and re-establishing my studio, my career has grown at an ever-increasing pace—video, cinema, books have all become part of my ever-expanding repertoire. My inspiration comes from all over but my true energy has always been here, and my years in Paris only helped to reinforce my belief that my creative force springs from the vitality of New York City.

ANTONIO LOPEZ

マイフレンズ, マイニューヨーク

私はプエルトリカンヒルズに囲まれた農園地ウチュアードで生まれた。両親の結婚は家同士の取り決めだったらしいが、その時母は14歳、父は17歳だったという。私が5歳になるまで家族はウチュアードで暮らした。当時のことは今でもはっきりと憶えている。2歳になると母のかたわらで絵を描いていた。母と一緒にドレスのスケッチをしたり、母がくれる残り布で洋服を作ったりしてよく遊んだ。不思議なことに父がひどく熱心だった。私がかんしゃくを起こすと野球のバットではなく人形を買ってくれたりした。その父が軍隊に徴兵されたために家族はウチュアードからサン・ファンに移った。それからは祖母と一緒に過ごす時間が多くなった。アメリカに来て初めて学校に入ったのが8歳のときだったから、それまで私は祖父母から読み書きを学んだことになる。

兄弟は弟が2人。私はいつもアメリカへ行くことを夢見ていた。ある時、父がフロリダの絵はがきを見せて、「これがニューヨークだ」と言った。花、熱帯植物、太陽の輝き。以来、私はニューヨークへ行きたくてたまらなくなった。そして気温零度のある夜、私はようやく憧れのニューヨークに着いた。だが、絵はがきとは似ても似つかぬ高いビルや、スパニッシュ・ハーレムの重苦しい雰囲気に、私はただただ呆然としてしまった。それでもじきにそこの暮らしに慣れてしまったが。

父はそのころ、マネキン人形を作る仕事をしていた。プラスター（粉末石膏）を型取り、彩色するその手際はびっくりするほどあざやかだった。学校から帰ると、父と一緒にマネキンに髪の毛を付ける仕事をよく手伝ったものである。母からはファッション、父からは人形を形づくり、仕上げるということを学んだ。素晴しいひとときであった。私の様々な思いつきが満たされてゆくのだ。野球とか、男の子なら誰でもするような遊びもするごく普通の少年だったが、家の方がずっと面白いといつも思っていた。

学校に行くときまって、いちばん綺麗な女の子と仲良くできた。女の子の気持ちが理解できたからだろう。他の男の子達がやたらと女の子をこわがらせたり、いじめたりしている中で、私は女の子が好きなものや、どうすれば女の子が喜ぶかを知っていた。だから人気があった。

初めて本当に私の世界とでも言うべきものに眼を向けさせてくれたのは母である。母は28歳の頃、花が咲き誇るように信じられないほど美しくなった。母は靴を集めていた。私は母が集めた靴に妄執とも言えるくらいの興味を示した。彼女はにじみ出るような女の魅力を持った女性だった。何もかもすっかり身に付いているといった風だった。ちょっとした心がけでいろんなことが出来るということを私は早くから母に学んだ。今でもそのことをよくモデル達に話す。

私はカトリック教徒として育てられたが、父が心霊術師でもあったため、白魔術の神秘的で特異な趣にも魅きつけられた。11歳の時ダンサーになろうと思いたち、1年間子供向けのショー番組に出てタップダンスを踊っていたこともあった。だが、それにもすぐあきてしまった私は、ドローイングという、自分がいちばん初めに魅せられたものへと戻っていった。そしてこの種のコンテストにことごとく優勝しては数々のメダルを手にするまでになった。先生達が口をそろえて私に絵描きになれと励ましてくれた。ハイスクールの頃、先生達の間から「そんなにドローイングがうまいのだから、ファッションイラストレーションをやってみてはどうか」という話が出た。デザインは後になっても学べるというわけである。同じような誘いが、ファッション・インスティテュート・オブ・テクノロジー（F. I. T.）からもあった。イラストレーション科にとの要望を受けて私はそこに籍を置くことにした。けれども、洋服のデザインをしたいという気持ちはいつも私の心のどこかしらにあった。

人間の体はもともとセクシーなものではないと思う。何か身にまとうことによって私達は魅力というものの存在に気づく。だから裸の状態ではイマジネーションが働かない。身に着けてこそ魅力が発揮されるという考え方は、おそらく異論の余地のないところであろう。服装は私達に様々な選択の可能性を与えてくれる。

私がたぶんに服飾デザインに魅かれていたのは、母がいつも実行したいと思いながら果たせなかった目的に、私が挑戦したいと思い続けていたからである。母への感謝なのかもしれない。これまで私はファッション・イラストレーションに打ちこみ、そして成功した。イラストでのゴールをきわめ、ファッション・デザインにも取り組める今、私は自分の力を美術の分野で生かしたいと思っている。

パリでの生活

パリのショールームでカール・ラガーフェルドと出会ったのは，1969年にエル誌の仕事で旅行した時のことである。スタジオを開設するためにパリに移って以来急速に親しくなり，お互いに行き来するようになった。カールは，サン・ジェルマンにアパートを見つけてくれた。しかしじきに私のアパートは住所不定のモデルやファッション界の有名人のアメリカンセンターになってしまった。パリに来るモデル達の多くは様々な理由でついにはパリに居ついてしまう。金がなくなって流れてきた者，ただパリという街を見てみたかっただけの者，新たな生活を夢見る者，色々である。そんな中でグレイス・ジョーンズ，エイジャ，ジェリー・ホール，パット・クリーブランド，ティナ・チョー，ジェシカ・ラングといった面々とは特に親しくしてきた。1960年代の後半はちょうどポップアートがフランス文化に影響を与え始めた頃だ。私は，この頃の感覚をファッション・イラストレーションに取り入れてみた。モデル達は再びホットパンツやスパイクロールを着るようになった。プラチナ・ブロンド，ブラック・ビューティが戻ってきたのである。

私達はこの流行に対して共通の感覚を持っていた。次に何が始まるのかという期待感で2人とも目を輝かせていた。そのころのカールはすでにパトロン的な存在だった。彼は私や友人であるドナ・ジョーダン，ジェーン・フォース，コリー・ティッピンらがパリやフレンチ・リビエラでも自分達のスタイルを表現できると確信していた。素晴しい日々だった。私達は，ラ・キューポラ，カフェ・フローラ，そして当時はまだ無名のクラブ・セブンといったカフェの社会とでも言うべきものに，さかんに新風を吹きこもうとしていた。ディスコと言う言葉が生まれる以前のことである。夜ごと外出してはバーが閉店するまで踊っていた。とりわけクラブ・セブンをひいきにしていたが，いつの間にか今のように有名になってしまった。アメリカのソウルミュージックに合わせて新しいダンスステップの工夫もした。フランス人はただリンディをするだけで，踊ることさえできなかった。私達がアメリカの文化を持ちこんだ。そして，カールを通じてアメリカの力を見せつけたのである。

夏が来ると，カールの借りたサント・ロペの大別荘へ，1等列車に乗っていった。（カールは何ヶ月も前から間違いなく予約を取ることができたのである）。青列車に乗り，専用の貨車に荷物を満載する。その中にはカールの最新ファッションも含まれていた。セルッティであつらえた洋服，ラリックをはじめパリでも最高級の店から集めた宝石類，シルクハット，ステッキ，パラソル。誰もがメイクアップをし，髪を長く伸ばし，少なくとも1日に3度は着替えをしたそんな頃である。タバ・ブランの，フラカスの，ジャック・フェスの入り乱れた香りが周囲に満ちていたそんな頃である。私達は自分達だけのリバを借り，ロールスロイスを乗りまわした。社交性と創造性への返礼として多くのものがおもちゃのように差し出された。親密な交友関係はこうしたことから伸展していったのである。

若さと感受性を満喫した日々だった。私達が世に送り出したモデルの中に，パティ・ダーバンヴィルがいる。当時まだ17歳だった。後にアンディ・ウォホールと知り合い，やがて彼の映画に出演するようになる。この頃出会ったモデル達はすごくいきいきして，生気に満ちていた。ある時私はパロマ・ピカソに翼をつけたような髪型をさせてみたことがある。2，3ヶ月するとまわりのモデル達が皆，その髪型で写真に写っているのだ。彼女達はたいがい最後にはギー・ブーディンか，ヘルムート・ニュートンと仕事をするようになった。1977年のイヴ・サン・ローランのコレクションでは5人のアメリカ人モデルが起用された。もちろん私が見つけてモデルにした娘達である。

とにかくよく働いたし，そして成長した。私達のつきあいは，アメリカに帰りたい気持ちが強くなり，カールが18世紀スタイルに関心を持ち始めた頃を境にして終わりを告げた。2人とも別々の道を歩き出したのだ。だが私達の友情には変わりがない。いまだに彼のことは家族の一員のような気がしている。

ニューヨークに戻ってスタジオを再設してからというもの，私の仕事は絶え間なく増え続けている。ビデオ，映画，本。私のレパートリーは拡大する一方である。インスピレーションはあらゆるものから生まれる。しかし，私の本来のエネルギーの生まれるところは，いつもニューヨークである。パリにおける数年間は，ただ私の信念を確かなものにしただけだった。私の創造的な力は，ここ，ニューヨークの活気の中からこそ湧いて出てくるのだという信念を。

アントニオ・ロペス

ANTONIO LOPEZ アントニオ・ロペス

Most Antonio Lopez captured the feeling of the times, giving us visual shocks in fashion each time. He is the super star of fashion art. (Pater Sato)

時代のフィーリングを誰よりも早く捉え，常にファッショナブルなビジュアル・ショックを与えてくれる。ファッションアートのスーパースター。（ペーター 佐藤）

グレース・ジョーンズ／ポートレイト／1983／水彩絵具，鉛筆／69×93cm

Grace Jones / Portrait / 1983 / Watercolor, pencil / 23″×31″
グレース・ジョーンズ／ポートレイト／1983／水彩絵具，鉛筆／69×93cm

TITLE   MEDIA
Angero / Portrait / 1983 / Watercolor, pencil / 23″ × 31″
アンジェロ/ポートレイト/1983/水彩絵具, 鉛筆/69×93cm

TITLE CLIENT MEDIA
Untitled / Vanity Fair / Editorial / 1984 / Watercolor, pencil / 19″ × 27″
無題/エディトリアル/1984/水彩絵具, 鉛筆/57×81cm

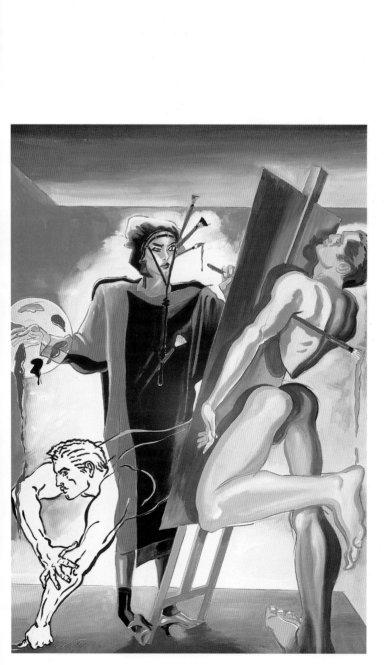

TITLE CLIENT MEDIA
Untitled / Vanity Fair / Editorial / 1984 / Watercolor, pencil / 19″ × 27″
無題/エディトリアル/1984/水彩絵具, 鉛筆/57×81cm

Marino / Portrait / 1983 / Watercolor, pencil / 23″×31″
マリーノ/ポートレイト/1983/水彩絵具、鉛筆/69×93cm

Untitled / G.Q. Magazine / Editorial / 1984 / Watercolor, pencil / 11″×14″
無題/エディトリアル/1984/水彩絵具, 鉛筆/33×42cm

Untitled / G.Q. Magazine / Editorial / 1984 / Watercolor, pencil / 11″×14″

無題／エディトリアル／1984／水彩絵具, 鉛筆／33×42cm

Untitled / G.Q. Magazine / Editorial / 1984 / Watercolor, pencil / 11″×14″
無題／エディトリアル／1984／水彩絵具，鉛筆／33×42cm

TITLE CLIENT MEDIA
Untitled / G.Q. Magazine / Editorial / 1984 / Watercolor, pencil / 11″×14″
無題/エディトリアル/1984/水彩絵具, 鉛筆/33×42cm

TITLE CLIENT MEDIA
Untitled / G.Q. Magazine / Editorial / 1984 / Watercolor, pencil / 11″×14″
無題/エディトリアル/1984/水彩絵具, 鉛筆/33×42cm

Untitled / G.Q. Magazine / Editorial / 1984 / Watercolor, pencil / 11″×14″
無題／エディトリアル／1984／水彩絵具，鉛筆／33×42cm

Untitled / G.Q. Magazine / Editorial / 1984 / Watercolor, pencil / 11″×14″
無題／エディトリアル／1984／水彩絵具，鉛筆／33×42cm

TITLE   CLIENT   MEDIA
Untitled / Vanity Fair / Editorial / 1984 / Watercolor, pencil / 19″×27″
無題／エディトリアル／1983／水彩絵具，鉛筆／57×84cm

TITLE   CLIENT   MEDIA
Untitled / Vanity / Editorial / 1983 / Watercolor, pencil / 18″×24″
無題/エディトリアル/1983/水彩絵具, 鉛筆/54×72cm

Untitled / Vanity / Editorial / 1983 / Watercolor, pencil / 18″×24″
無題／エディトリアル／1983／水彩絵具，鉛筆／54×72cm

Untitled / Vanity / Editorial / 1983 / Watercolor, pencil / 18″×24″
無題／エディトリアル／1983／水彩絵具，鉛筆／54×72cm

Untitled / Vanity / Editorial / 1983 / Watercolor, pencil / 18″ × 24″
無題/エディトリアル/1983/水彩絵具, 鉛筆/54×72cm

Untitled / Vanity / Editorial / 1983 / Watercolor, pencil / 18″ × 24″
無題/エディトリアル/1983/水彩絵具, 鉛筆/54×72cm

TITLE   CLIENT   MEDIA
Untitled / Bloomingdale's / N.Y. Times / 1983 / Pencil / 18″×24″
無題／雑誌／1983／鉛筆／54×72cm

Untitled / Bloomingdale's / N.Y. Times / 1983 / Pencil / 18″ × 24″

無題/雑誌/1983/鉛筆/54×72cm

JIM HOWARD ジム・ハワード

In his illustration of clothing, Howard's use of texture is outstanding. It is as if the models are alive. Influence of American realism is clearly evident. (Pater Sato)

服のテクスチュアの表現が素晴らしい。描かれた人物の存在感，アメリカン・リアリズムの流れを感じさせる。トラディッショナル派。(ペーター佐藤)

Line-Up / Hudson's / Magazine / 1982 / Charcoal, graphite + wash on paper
並んで/雑誌/1982/チャコール，グラファイト鉛筆，画用紙。ウォッシュ

Jewels / Bonwit Teller / Magazine / 1977 / Charcoal, graphite + wash on paper / 13″×16″
宝石/雑誌/1977/チャコール，グラファイト鉛筆，画用紙。ウォッシュ/39×48cm

The Compulsion in my work is to draw better, to grow and stretch as an artist, to bring more good classical art into my work. Hopefully improving the quality of the fashion art showcase. My love is art—I love to draw. (Jim Howard)

いつも心がけているのはより良く描き，アーティストとして成長しようとする姿勢です。その際作品に過去のすぐれた芸術作品の良いところをとり入れようとしています。ファッションアートの向上に自分が役立てばと思います。本当に描くことが好きですから。（ジム・ハワード）

His + Hers / Bonwit Teller / Newspaper / 1977 / Charcoal, graphite + wash on paper / 20″ tall
彼と彼女の/新聞/1977/チャコール，グラファイト鉛筆，画用紙。ウォッシュ/縦60cm

Boots / B. Altman / Newspaper / 1982 / Charcoal, graphite + wash on paper / 16″ tall
ブーツ/新聞/1982/チャコール，グラファイト鉛筆，画用紙。ウォッシュ/縦48cm

Shipboard / Garfinkles / Newspaper / 1984 / Charcoal, graphite + wash on paper / 13″×18″
船上/新聞/1984/チャコール，グラファイト鉛筆，画用紙。ウォッシュ/39×54cm

TITLE   CLIENT   MEDIA
Champaign / Garfinkles / Newspaper / 1984 / Charcoal, graphite + wash on paper / 15″ × 20″
シャンペン/新聞/1984/チャコール, グラファイト鉛筆, 画用紙。ウォッシュ/45×60cm

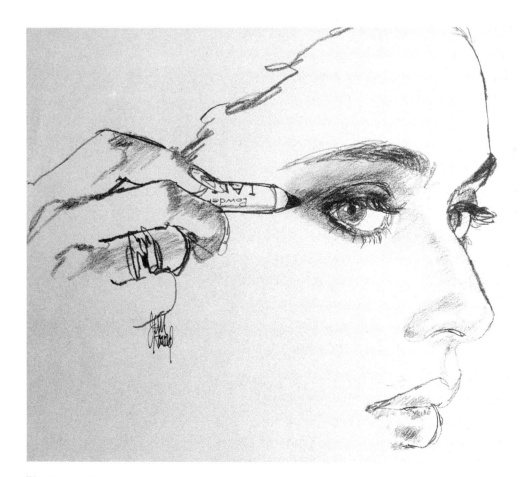

TITLE   CLIENT   MEDIA
Hats / B. Altman / Newspaper / 1983 / Charcoal, graphite + wash on paper / 13″ × 17″
帽子/新聞/1983/チャコール, グラファイト鉛筆, 画用紙。ウォッシュ/39×51cm

TITLE   CLIENT   MEDIA
Eyes / B. Altman / Newspaper / 1984 / Charcoal, graphite + wash on paper / 10″ tall
瞳/新聞/1984/チャコール, グラファイト鉛筆, 画用紙。ウォッシュ/縦30cm

Nailpolish / Bonwit Teller / Newspaper / 1978 / Charcoal, graphite + wash on paper / 14″ tall
マニュキア/新聞/1978/チャコール, グラファイト鉛筆, 画用紙。ウォッシュ/縦42cm

Male / Bonwit Teller / Newspaper / 1978 / Charcoal, graphite + wash on paper / 14″ tall
男/新聞/1978/チャコール, グラファイト鉛筆, 画用紙。ウォッシュ/縦42cm

Fur Jacket / B. Altman / Newspaper / 1983 / Charcoal, graphite + wash on paper / 13″ tall
毛皮のジャケット/新聞/1983/チャコール, グラファイト鉛筆, 画用紙。ウォッシュ/縦39cm

Stripes / B. Altman / Newspaper / 1984 / Charcoal, graphite + wash on paper / 18″ tall
ストライプ/新聞/1984/チャコール, グラファイト鉛筆, 画用紙。ウォッシュ/縦54cm

Perry's / B. Altman / Newspaper / 1982 / Charcoal, graphite + wash on paper / 23″ tall
ペリーズ/新聞/1982/チャコール, グラファイト鉛筆, 画用紙。ウォッシュ/縦69cm

Stripes II / B. Altman / Newspaper / 1983 / Charcoal, graphite + wash on paper / 21″ tall
ストライプⅡ/新聞/1983/チャコール, グラファイト, 画用紙。ウォッシュ/縦63cm

Willi's / B. Altman / Newspaper / 1983 / Charcoal, graphite + wash on paper / 18″ tall
ウィリーズ/新聞/1983/チャコール, グラファイト鉛筆, 画用紙。ウォッシュ/縦54cm

PEDRO BARRIOS ペドロ・バリオス

Freedom, ease, subtleness. Elegant forms are expressed in a few well-chosen lines. Barrios has allowed us to appreciate authentic beauty once again. (Pater Sato)

繊細で洒脱。選ばれた線の美しさ，フォルムの美しさは無類。オーセンティックな美を再認識させてくれる。（ペーター佐藤）

TITLE CLIENT
Tigerman / Norma Kamali / 1982 / Watercolor on paper / 19″ × 24″
タイガーマン/1982/水彩絵具，画用紙/57×72cm

Talent is nice. Discipline, research studies, and lots of hard work are indispensable. The conviction of doing better the next time is neccessary, don't fall in love with the last work or you'll never be better. (Pedro Barrios)

才能があることも大切ですが，訓練，洞察，勤勉さなどは欠くことのできない要素だと思います。次はもっといいものを描こうとする信念が大切です。出来上がってしまった作品にほれこんではいけません。でないと決して上にはいけません。(ペドロ・バリオス)

Swan / Norma Kamali / W.W.D. / 1982 / Pen & ink / 19″ × 24″
スワン/新聞/1982/ペン，インク/57×72cm

Lady / Norma Kamali / 1982 / Pen & ink / 19″ × 24″
レディ/1982/ペン，インク/57×72cm

31

TITLE   CLIENT   MEDIA
Red / Bloomingdale's / Catalog / 1983 / Acrylic, pen & ink / 19″ × 24″
レッド/カタログ/1983/アクリル絵具, ペン, インク/57×72cm

TITLE   CLIENT   MEDIA
Cross / Bloomingdale's / Catalog / 1983 / Acrylic, pen & ink / 19″ × 24″
クロス/カタログ/1983/アクリル絵具, ペン, インク/57×72cm

Bathing Suit / Bloomingdale's / N.Y. Times / 1984 / Acrylic, pen & ink / 19″ × 20″
水着/新聞/1984/アクリル絵具, ペン, インク/57×60cm

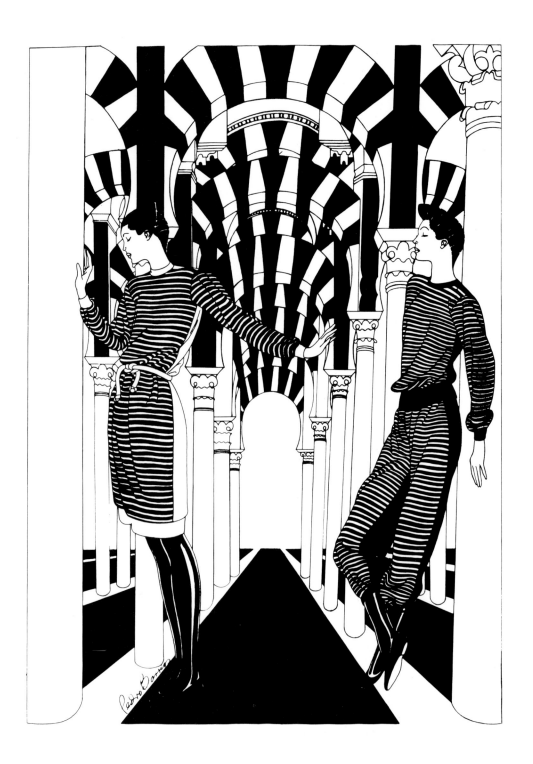

TITLE CLIENT MEDIA
2 Lady Stripe / Bloomingdale's / N.Y. Times / 1983 / Acrylic,
pen & ink / 19″×24″
2 レディストライプ／新聞／1983／アクリル絵具，ペン，インク／57×72cm

TITLE CLIENT MEDIA
4 Head / Bloomingdale's / N.Y. Times / 1984 / Acrylic, pen & ink / 22″×15″
4つの頭／新聞／1984／アクリル絵具，ペン，インク／66×45cm

TITLE   CLIENT   MEDIA
3 Lady Sailer / Bloomingdale's / N.Y. Times / 1983 / Acrylic, pen & ink / 19″ × 24″
3 レディセイラー/新聞/1983/アクリル絵具, ペン, インク/57×72cm

TITLE   CLIENT   MEDIA
3 Figure / Bloomingdale's / N.Y. Times / 1984 / Acrylic, pen & ink / 24″ ×19″
3人/新聞/1984/アクリル絵具, ペン, インク/72×57cm

J. CRAWFORD J.クロフォード

Crawford is able to capture the necessary sense of speed and movement in his newspaper illustration. The tone and contrast of black and white are effective. (Pater Sato)

スピード感のある線の走り，新聞広告を手がけているだけに，黒と白のコントラストや調子が効果的である。(ペーター佐藤)

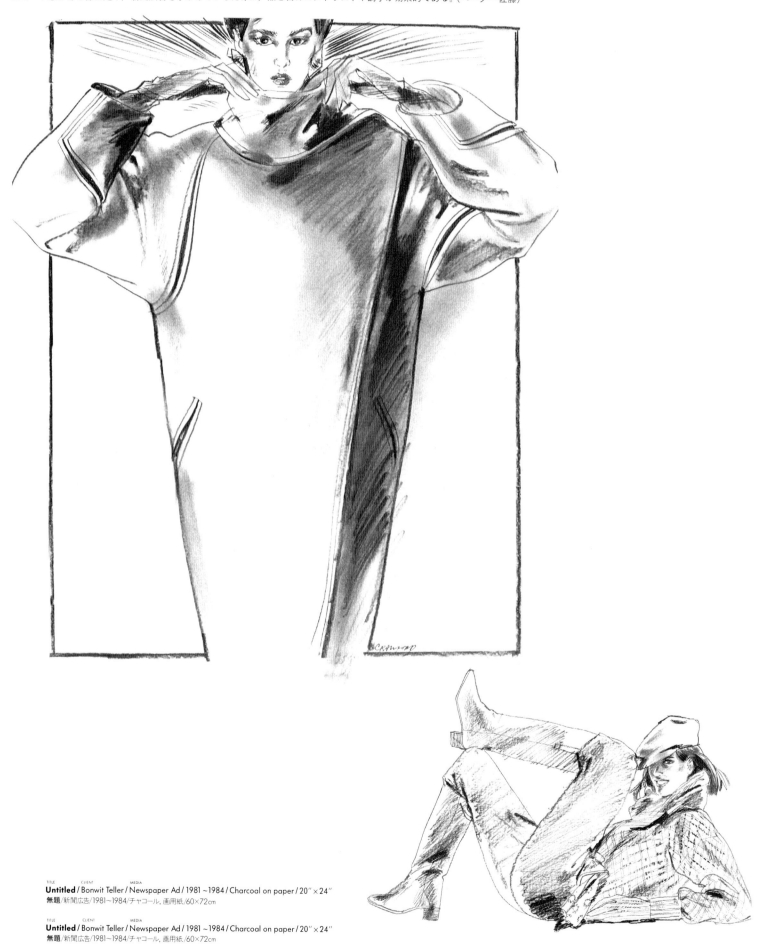

TITLE   CLIENT   MEDIA
Untitled/Bonwit Teller/Newspaper Ad/1981~1984/Charcoal on paper/20"×24"
無題/新聞広告/1981~1984/チャコール, 画用紙/60×72cm

TITLE   CLIENT   MEDIA
Untitled/Bonwit Teller/Newspaper Ad/1981~1984/Charcoal on paper/20"×24"
無題/新聞広告/1981~1984/チャコール, 画用紙/60×72cm

Try to make most of attitude & mood of model & garment—look for the unusual aspects to be found in placement on page and dramatic light & shadow. (J. Crawford)

モデルと服のおおよその雰囲気をつかむようにしてください。ページの中に一味ちがった要素を盛りこむこと。ドラマチックな光と影を表現することに気を配るといいと思います。（J. クロフォード）

Untitled / Bonwit Teller / Newspaper Ad / 1981 ~1984 / Charcoal on paper / 20″ × 24″
無題/新聞広告/1981~1984/チャコール, 画用紙/60×72cm

Untitled / Bonwit Teller / Newspaper Ad / 1981 ~1984 / Charcoal on paper / 20″ × 24″
無題/新聞広告/1981~1984/チャコール, 画用紙/60×72cm

Untitled / Bonwit Teller / Newspaper Ad / 1981 ~1984 / Charcoal on paper / 20″ × 24″
無題/新聞広告/1981~1984/チャコール, 画用紙/60×72cm

Untitled / Bonwit Teller / Newspaper Ad / 1981 ~1984 / Charcoal on paper / 20″ × 24″
無題/新聞広告/1981~1984/チャコール, 画用紙/60×72cm

TITLE CLIENT MEDIA
Untitled / Bonwit Teller / Newspaper Ad / 1981 ~1984 / Charcoal on paper / 20″ × 24″
無題/新聞広告/1981~1984/チャコール, 画用紙/60×72cm

TITLE CLIENT MEDIA
Untitled / Bonwit Teller / Newspaper Ad / 1981 ~1984 / Charcoal on paper / 20″ × 24″
無題/新聞広告/1981~1984/チャコール, 画用紙/60×72cm

TITLE CLIENT MEDIA
Untitled / Bonwit Teller / Newspaper Ad / 1981 ~1984 / Charcoal on paper / 20″ × 24″
無題/新聞広告/1981~1984/チャコール, 画用紙/60×72cm

TITLE CLIENT MEDIA
Untitled / Bonwit Teller / Newspaper Ad / 1981 ~1984 / Charcoal on paper / 20″ × 24″
無題/新聞広告/1981~1984/チャコール, 画用紙/60×72cm

TITLE　CLIENT　MEDIA
Untitled / Bonwit Teller / Newspaper Ad / 1981 ~ 1984 / Charcoal on paper / 20″×24″
無題/新聞広告/1981~1984/チャコール, 画用紙/60×72cm

TITLE　CLIENT　MEDIA
Untitled / Bonwit Teller / Newspaper Ad / 1981 ~ 1984 / Charcoal on paper / 20″×24″
無題/新聞広告/1981~1984/チャコール, 画用紙/60×72cm

TITLE · CLIENT · MEDIA
Untitled / Bonwit Teller / Newspaper Ad / 1981 ~1984 / Charcoal on paper / 20″ × 24″
無題／新聞広告／1981~1984／チャコール, 画用紙／60×72cm

Untitled / Bonwit Teller / Newspaper Ad / 1981 ~1984 / Charcoal on paper / 20″ × 24″
無題／新聞広告／1981~1984／チャコール, 画用紙／60×72cm

WILLIAM RIESER ウィリアム・リーサー

William Rieser's touch is thrilling. He is a new talent bursting out from the New Wave sensation of the 80's. (Pater Sato)
80年代のニューウェーブ感覚で躍り出た新しい才能。スリリングなタッチが新鮮。(ペーター佐藤)

TITLE   CLIENT
Masked Man / Standard Brands / 1984 / Cut paper, pastel, pencil / 20″×20″
マスクマン/1984/カットペーパー, パステル, 鉛筆/60×60cm

Untitled / Standard Brands / Display / 1984 / Pantone, pastel, pencil / 18″×24″
無題／ディスプレイ／1984／パントーン・フィルム，パステル，鉛筆／54×72cm

泳ぐ人／ディスプレイ／1984／パントーン・フィルム，パステル，鉛筆／54×72cm

Swimmer / Standard Brands / Dispaly / 1984 / Pantone, pastel, pencil / 18″×24″
泳ぐ人／ディスプレイ／1984／パントーン・フィルム，パステル，鉛筆／54×72cm

Untitled / Kasparians / Promotion / 1983 / Pencil, Pantone, pastel / 20″×20″
無題/プロモーション/1983/鉛筆，パントーン・フィルム，パステル/60×60cm

Fred / Britches Magazine / Magazine / 1981 / Pencil / 19″×24″
フレッド/雑誌/1981/鉛筆/57×72cm

Levis Cords / Unpublished / 1983 / Pastel, pencil, Pantone / 22″×26″
リーバイスのコーデュロイ／未発表作品／パステル, 鉛筆, パントーン・フィルム／66×78cm

TITLE CLIENT MEDIA
Untitled / Lois Sportswear / Magazine Ad / 1983 / Pencil, chalk, Pantone / 22″ × 24″
無題／雑誌広告／1983／鉛筆, チョーク, パントーン・フィルム／66×72cm

TITLE CLIENT MEDIA
Untitled / Lois Sportswear / Magazine Ad / 1983 / Pastel, pencil, Pantone / 22″ × 24″
無題／雑誌広告／1983／パステル, 鉛筆, パントーン・フィルム／66×72cm

Untitled / Lois Sportswear / Magazine Ad / 1984 / Watercolor, pencil, pastel / 26″×32″
無題/雑誌広告/1984/水彩絵具, 鉛筆, パントーン・フィルム/78×96cm

Untitled / Macy's / Brochure / 1983 / Pastel / 18″×23″
無題/パンフレット/1983/パステル/54×69cm

DAVID CROLAND デビッド・クローランド

David Croland's dazzling originality can be sensed in his refined extravagances in which he superbly blends sensualism with expressionism. (Pater Sato)

感覚と表現の見事な融合。洗練された奔放さに強烈なオリジナリティーを感じさせる。（ペーター 佐藤）

TITLE
Make-Up / 1984 / Pastel / 14″×17″
メイクアップ／1984／パステル／42×51cm

TITLE
Beauty / 1984 / Pastel / 14″×17″
ビューティ／1984／パステル／42×51cm

TITLE
Shoe / 1983 / Pastel / 14″×17″
靴/1984//パステル/42×51cm

TITLE
Summer Beauty / 1983 / Pastel / 14″×17″
サマー・ビューティ/1983/パステル/42×51cm

TITLE
Shades / 1984 / Pastel / 14″×17″
サングラス / 1984 / パステル / 42×51cm

TITLE
Beach Nap / 1984 / Pastel / 14″×17″
ビーチの午睡 / 1984 / パステル / 42×51cm

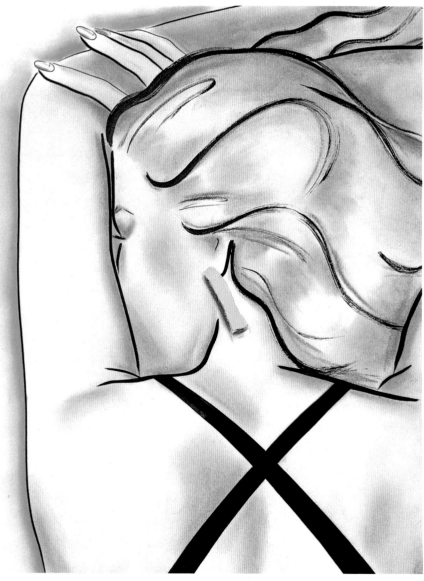

TITLE   CLIENT
Untitled / Revron / 1982 / Pastel / 14″×17″
無題／1982／パステル／42×51cm

TITLE
Girl / 1983 / Pastel / 14″×17″
ガール／1983／パステル／42×51cm

TITLE
Zebra Girl / 1983 / Pastel / 14″×17″
ゼブラ・ガール／1983／パステル／42×51cm

TITLE
Jungle / 1983 / Pastel / 14″×17″
ジャングル／1983／パステル／42×51cm

TITLE
Fur / 1983 / Pastel / 14″×17″
毛皮／1983／パステル／42×51cm

TITLE   CLIENT   MEDIA
Untitled / Bloomingdale's / N.Y. Times / 1983 / Pastel / 14″×17″
無題/雑誌/1983/パステル/42×51cm

TITLE   CLIENT   MEDIA
Untitled / Berdorf Goodman / N.Y. Times / 1983 / Pencil / 14″×17″
無題/雑誌/1983/鉛筆/42×51cm

GEORGE STAVRINOS ジョージ・スタヴリノス

Skillful at achieving a preciseness in his forms and in contrasting shades of black and white. George Stavrinos is the foremost in pencil illustration. Recently, his work has been simple with calculating precision reaching a stage of mellowness. (Pater Sato)

フォルムの確かさと，白と黒のコントラストの妙。ペンシル画の第一人者だ。最近のシンプルで計算のいきとどいた表現は円熟の境地に達している。(ペーター佐藤)

Mystery And Identity / Chrysler Museum / Poster for exhibit / 1984 / Watercolor, colored pencil, and graphite on Strathmore paper / 20″×27″
ミステリーとアイデンティティ/展示会用ポスター/1984/水彩絵具, 色鉛筆, グラファイト鉛筆/ストラスモア紙/60×84cm

54

I came to N.Y.C. in 1973 to see if I could find work as an illustrator (although my art training was in graphics). My first work was with the N.Y. Times for the book review and magazine sections. Within six months I joined Pushpin Studios on a freelance basis for 3-1/2 years. Near the end of that period, I began doing editorial fashion drawings for various magazines. From this, I became known for my ''Fashion illustrations''—first doing advertising for Barney's, then Bergdorf Goodman. My career as a fashion illustrator was actually quite by accident! (George Stavrinos)

1973年にイラストレーターとして働きたいと思ってニューヨークにやってきました（それまではグラフィックデザインを勉強していました）。最初の作品はニューヨークタイムズの書評欄と雑誌ページに掲載されました。それから６ヶ月後，プッシュピンスタジオに参加し，フリーランスのイラストレーターとして３年半活動しました。プッシュピン時代の終わりごろには，様々な雑誌のエディトリアル・ファッションドローイングを手がけるようになっていたのです。それ以来私は，ファッションイラストレーターとして認められるようになりました。バーニーズ，ボーグドルフ・グッドマンの広告を手がけたのがこの分野での最初の仕事です。私のファッションイラストレーターとしての経歴はこのように全く偶然によるものなのです！（ジョージ・スタヴリノス）

BERGDORF GOODMAN
GEOFFREY BEENE

TITLE / CLIENT / MEDIA
Female Head / Clinique Cosmetics / Newspaper (Europe) / 1983 / Pencil on Arches paper / 15″×12″
女の頭/新聞/1983/鉛筆, 水彩画紙/45×36cm

TITLE / CLIENT / MEDIA
Figure In Quilted Jacket / Bergdorf Goodman / N.Y. Times / 1983 / Pencil on Arches paper / 17″×21″
キルトジャケット/新聞/1983/鉛筆, 水彩画紙/51×63cm

Quilted Jacket / Klopman Fabrics / Test Ad / 1979 / Watercolor, colored pencil, and graphite on Strathmore paper / 20″ ×12″
キルトジャケット/テストアド/1979/水彩絵具, 色鉛筆, グラファイト鉛筆, ストラスモア紙, 60×36cm

The Bather / Gentlemen's Quarterly / G.Q. Magazine / 1977 / Watercolor, colored pencil, and graphite on Strathmore paper / 10″ ×10″
水浴び/雑誌/1977/水彩絵具, 色鉛筆, グラファイト鉛筆, ストラスモア紙/30×30cm

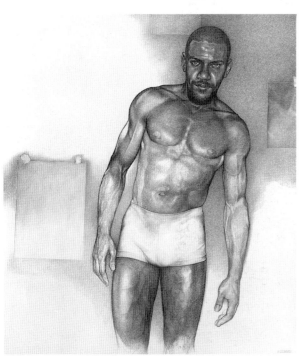

TITLE   CLIENT   MEDIA
Man At Window / Barney's / New Yorker Magazine / 1978 / Pencil on Arches paper / 9″ × 8″
窓辺の男/雑誌/1978/鉛筆, 水彩画紙/27×24cm

TITLE
Standing Male Figure / 1981 / Pencil on Arches paper / 23″ × 25″
立っている男/1981/鉛筆, 水彩画紙/69×75cm

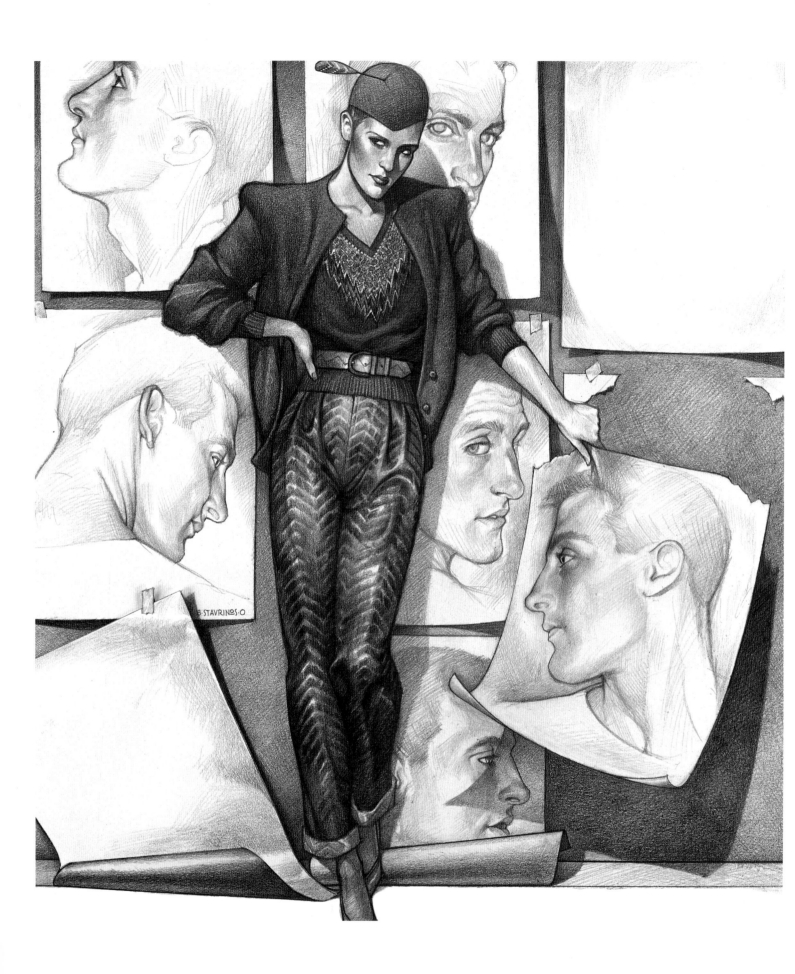

Figure With 6 Portraits / Bergdorf Goodman / N.Y. Times / 1980 / Pencil on Arches paper / 15″×17″
6枚のポートレイト/新聞/1980/鉛筆, 水彩画紙/45×51cm

Figure With Sphere / Bergdorf Goodman / N.Y. Times / 1980 / Pencil on Arches paper / 15″×15″
球体/新聞/1980/鉛筆, 水彩画紙/45×45cm

Figure With Torn Letter / Bergdorf Goodman / N.Y. Times / 1979 / Pencil on Arches paper / 15″×15″
引き裂かれた手紙/新聞/1979/鉛筆, 水彩画紙/45×45cm

KICHISABURO OGAWA キチサブロー・オガワ

Kichisaburo Ogawa is the foremost Japanese illustrator using the W.W.D. paper as his stage. His streak lines are simple and pure emitting a clean feeling. (Pater Sato)

ＷＷＤ紙を舞台に活躍している随一の日本人アーティスト。ストイックな線にさっぱりとした清潔感を感じる。(ペーター 佐藤)

TITLE   CLIENT   MEDIA
Untitled / W.W.D. / Newspaper / 1983 / Pen, color pen / 13″×16″
無題/新聞/1983/ペン，カラーペン/39×48cm

TITLE   CLIENT   MEDIA
Untitled / W.W.D. / Newspaper / 1983 / Color pen, color paper / 10″×13″
無題/新聞/1983/カラーペン，カラーペーパー/30×39cm

I like a word "Simple". When I sit on chair front of desk, and try to draw a illustration, I'm always considering to draw as simple as possible. (Kichisaburo Ogawa)

"シンプル"という言葉が好きです。机に向かって作品を描こうとするとき，いつもできるだけシンプルに描くことを心がけています。（キチサブロー・オガワ）

Untitled / W.W.D. / Newspaper / 1984 / Pen, color pen, color paper / 12″×17″

無題／新聞／1984／ペン，カラーペン，カラーペーパー／36×51cm

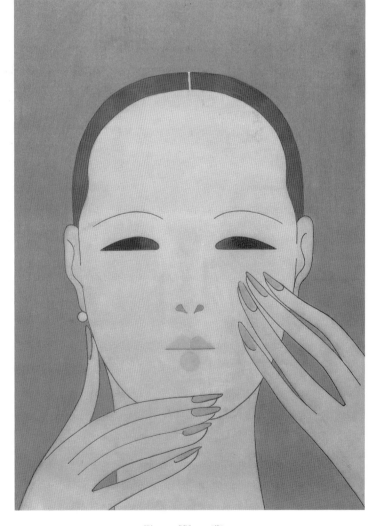

Untitled / W.W.D. / Newspaper / 1984 / Pen, color pen / 10″×13″

無題／新聞／1984／ペン，カラーペン／30×39cm

MICHAEL VAN HORN マイケル・ヴァン・ホーン

Michael Van Horn's use of curved lines in his pencil drawings is wonderfully enchanting. (Pater Sato)
曲線を駆使したペンシル画は妙になまめかしさを感じさせる。（ペーター佐藤）

Ralph Lauren / Filene's / W. / 1983 / Watercolor / 17″×17″
ラルフ・ローレン／新聞／1983／水彩絵具／51×51cm

TITLE   CLIENT   MEDIA
Ann Kline / Filene's / Boston Globe / 1983 / Watercolor / 17″×17″
アン・クライン/雑誌/1983/水彩絵具/51×51cm

TITLE   CLIENT   MEDIA
Norma Kamali / Filene's / Boston Globe / 1983 / Watercolor / 17″×17″
ノーマ・カマリ/雑誌/1983/水彩絵具/51×51cm

TITLE **Elizabeth de Senneville** CLIENT / Filene's / Boston Globe / MEDIA 1983 / Watercolor / 17″×17″
エリザベス・ド・セネヴィル/雑誌/1983/水彩絵具/51×51cm

TITLE   CLIENT   MEDIA
Jackie Rogers / Filene's / Boston Globe / 1983 / Watercolor / 17″×17″
ジャッキー・ロジャース/雑誌/1983/水彩絵具/51×51cm

TITLE   CLIENT   MEDIA
Bill Blass / Filene's / Boston Globe / 1983 / Watercolor / 17″×17″
ビル・ブラス/雑誌/1983/水彩絵具/51×51cm

TITLE CLIENT MEDIA
Girbaud/ Filene's / Boston Globe/ 1984 / Watercolor / 17″ ×17″
ギルボウド/雑誌/1984/水彩絵具/51×51cm

TITLE   CLIENT   MEDIA
Jr. Japanese / Filene's / Boston Globe / 1983 / Watercolor / 17″×17″
ジュニア・ジャパニーズ/雑誌/1983/水彩絵具/51×51cm

MARTIN HOFFMAN マーティン・ホフマン

There is no one on the same level as Martin Hoffman in men's fashion illustrations. His brilliant sensitivity can be evidenced in his concentrated technique. (Pater Sato)

男性ファッションを描いたらこの人の右に出る人がいるだろうか。コンセントレートされたテクニックに感性の冴えをみる。(ペーター佐藤)

Basile / L Uomo Vogue / 1983～1984 / Various pastel / 20″×30″
バジル/雑誌/1983～1984/パステル/60×90cm

TITLE　MEDIA
Basile / Italian Vogue / 1983~1984 / Various pastel / 20″×30″
バジル/雑誌/1983~1984//パステル/60×90cm

Jean Paul German / Playboy / 1983~1984 / Various pastel / 20″×30″
ジャン・ポール・ジャルマン／雑誌／1983~1984／パステル／60×90cm

TITLE　　　　MEDIA
Basile / L Uomo Vogue / 1983~1984 / Various pastel / 20″×30″

バジル/雑誌/1983~1984//パステル/60×90cm

Gil Truedson / Playboy / 1983~1984 / Various pastel / 20″×30″
ギル・トルードソン/雑誌/1983~1984//パステル/60×90cm

Basile / L Uomo Vogue / 1983~1984 / Various pastel / 20″×30″
バジル/雑誌/1983~1984/パステル/60×90cm

Basile / L Uomo Vogue / 1983〜1984 / Pastel / 20″×30″

バジル/雑誌/1983〜1984/パステル/60×90cm

Alexander Julian / Playboy / 1983〜1984 / Various pastel / 20″×30″

アレクサンダー・ジュリアン/雑誌/1983〜1984/パステル/60×90cm

Classic / Illust. Magazine, Japan / 1983~1984 / Pastel / 20″×30″
クラシック/雑誌//パステル/60×90cm

Nippon / Unpublished / 1983~1984 / Pastel, acrylic / 20″×30″
ニッポン/未発表作品/1983~1984/パステル、アクリル絵具/60×90cm

HARVEY BOYD ハービー・ボイド

Harvey Boyd has a unique sense of style. Although his styles has changed recently, it is characterized by his unusual sence of beauty. (Pater Sato)

ひとくせある独特のテースト。最近スタイルを変えたが，常にひと味違う美意識につらぬかれている。（ペーター佐藤）

TITLE MEDIA
Rhythm #1 / Unpublished / 1983 / Charcoal on self adhesive paper / 18″×24″
リズム#1/未発表作品/1983/チャコール/54×72 cm

TITLE MEDIA
Rhythm #2 / Unpublished / 1983 / Pastel stick on dots / 18″×24″
リズム#2/未発表作品/1983/パステル/54×72cm

TITLE · MEDIA
Rhythm ＃4/ Unpublished / 1983 / Pastel stick on dots / 18″×20″
リズム#4/未発表作品/1983//パステル/54×60cm

TITLE · MEDIA
Rhythm ＃3/ Unpublished / 1983 / Pastel stick on dots / 18″×24″
リズム#3/未発表作品/1983//パステル/54×72cm

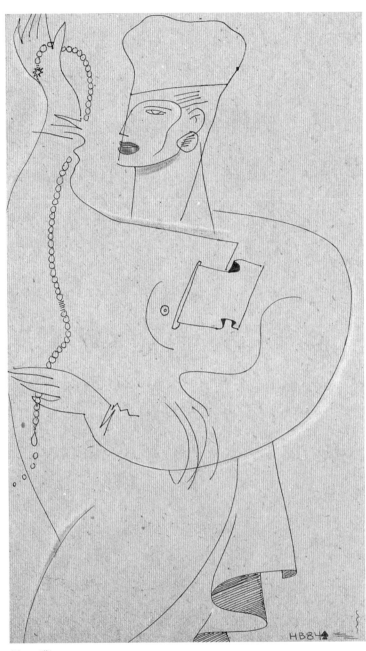

TITLE　　　MEDIA
Pearls / Unpublished / 1983 / Pen, colored pencil / 8″×11″
パール/未発表作品/1983/ペン, 色鉛筆/24×33cm

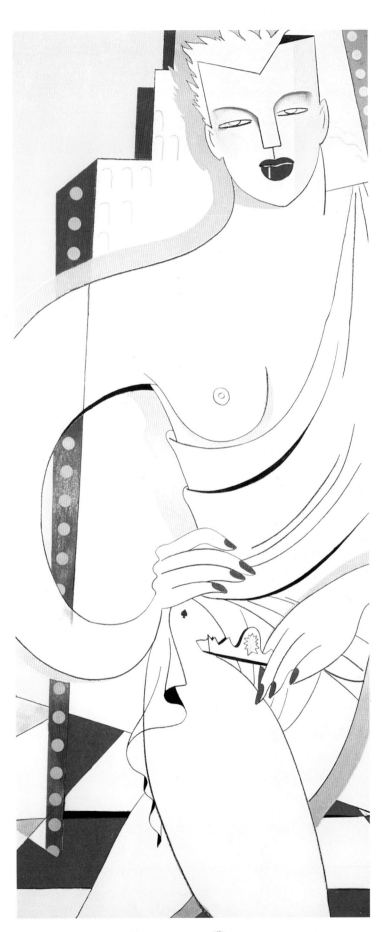

TITLE　　　　　　　　　MEDIA
Summer In New York / Unpublished / 1983 / Pastel stick on dots / 3′×9′
ニューヨークの夏/未発表作品/1983/パステル/90×270cm

Untitled / N.Y. Times / Magazine / 1980 / Pen, colored pencil
無題/雑誌/1983/ペン, 色鉛筆

Untitled / W.W.D. / Promotion / 1983 / Pen, colored pencil
無題/プロモーション/1983/ペン, 色鉛筆

Young Man / Unpublished / 1983 / Pen, colored pencil / 18″×24″
若者/未発表作品/1983/ペン, 色鉛筆/54×27cm

Adel Bertei / Warner Brothers / Record Album / 1983 / Pen, colored pencil / 16″×16″
アデル・ベルテ/レコードジャケット/1983/ペン, 色鉛筆/48×48cm

MATS GUSTAVSON マッツ・グスタブソン

Using simple lines with no waste, Mats Gustavson wins fantastic reviews in the fashion world. They are so wonderful to provoke jealousy in other illustrators. (Pater Sato)

無駄のないシンプルな表現で，ファッションのポイントを摑む感覚は抜群。ジェラシーを感じさせるほどうまい。（ペーター佐藤）

TITLE   CLIENT
Leg/Vogue Beauté/1983/Pastel/40″×30″
レッグ/雑誌/1983//パステル/120×90cm

TITLE
Fashions of the Times / N.Y. Times / Magazine Cover / 1984 / Pastel / 40″ × 30″
ファッションズ・オブ・ザ・タイムス/雑誌の表紙/1984/パステル/120×90cm

Violet intense
et couleurs
chaudes pour
ce maquillage
d'Estée
Lauder. Sur
les paupières,
Automatic
Crème
Eyeshadow
"Horizon
Blue" et
Pressed Eyelid
Shadow
"Terra Cotta".
Sur les
joues : Tender
Blusher
"Brandied
Coral". Lèvres :
Polished
Performance
"Riviera Red".

TITLE CLIENT MEDIA
Untitled / Marie Claire / Editorial / 1980 / Pastel / 14″×17″
無題／エディトリアル／1980／パステル／42×51cm

NORMA KAMALI

X-silhuett
åtsittande fodral
avskurna axlar
getingmidja
tydliga hofter
mycket stjärt
vidd från knaet
hoga vrister

X trem glamour

Norma Kamali / Clic Magazine (Sweden) / Editorial / 1983 / Pastel / 40″ × 30″
ノーマ・カマリ/エディトリアル/1983/パステル/120×90 cm

TITLE
Lou Lattimore / Lou Lattimore / Invitation Card / 1983 / Pastel / 40″×30″
ルー・ラティモア/招待状/1983/パステル/120×90cm

TITLE | CLIENT | MEDIA
Claude Montana / Marie Claire, Bis / Magazine Cover / 1983 / Pencil, pastel / 40″×30″
クロード・モンタナ／雑誌の表紙／1983／鉛筆, パステル／120×90cm

TITLE | CLIENT | MEDIA
Thierry Mugler / Marie Claire, Bis / Editorial / 1983 / Pencil, pastel / 40″×30″
ティエリー・ミュグレー／エディトリアル／1983／鉛筆, パステル／120×90cm

TITLE   CLIENT   MEDIA
Alaïa / Lou Lattimore / Advertising / 1983 / Pastel / 40″ × 40″
アライア/広告/1983//パステル/120×120cm

TITLE   CLIENT   MEDIA
Untitled / Lou Lattimore / Advertising / 1983 / Pastel / 40″ × 40″
無題/広告/1983/パステル/120×120cm

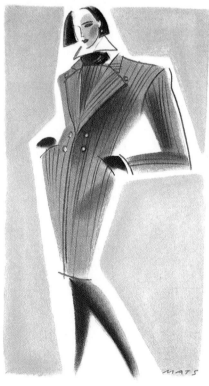

JOEL RESNICOFF ジョエル・レズニコフ

Joel Resnicoff sends us messages of joy, peace, and humor. His comic style shows us a new world. (Pater Sato)
ハッピネス，ユーモア，ピースフル。そんなメッセージが伝わってくる。コミックス調のスタイルで新境地を見せてくれる。（ペーター佐藤）

To believe in yourself and to always go for the dream. (Joel Resnicoff)
自分自身を信じ夢を追いかけることです。(ジョエル・レズニコフ)

TITLE
Summer Fun / 1980 / Charcoal, dyes / 14″×17″
サマー・ファン/1980/チャコール,カラーインク/42×51cm

TITLE   MEDIA
Armani Fall '84 / Vanity Magazine / 1984 / Charcoal, gouache / 18″×24″
アルマーニ・秋 '84/雑誌/1984/チャコール,ガッシュ/54×72cm

U.S. Wear / Macy's / 1984 / Charcoal, gouache / 12″ × 22″
USウェア/1984/チャコール, ガッシュ/36×66cm

Tassha / Macy's / 1983 / Charcoal, gouache / 11″ × 22″
タシャ/1983/チャコール, ガッシュ/33×66cm

TITLE
St. Laurent Fall / 1981 / Charcoal, gouache / 18″ × 24″
サンローラン・秋 /1981/ チャコール, ガッシュ /54×72cm

93

Tokyo Spirit / Village Voice / 1983 / Charcoal, gouache / 18″ × 24″
トーキョー・スピリット/新聞/1983/チャコール, ガッシュ/54×72cm

Kagome Tomato Juice / Kagome / Japanese magazine / 1983 / Charcoal, gouache / 14″ ×17″
カゴメ・トマトジュース/雑誌/1983/チャコール, ガッシュ/42×51cm

To Dye For / Village Voice / 1983 / Charcoal, gouache / 18″×24″
染める/新聞/1983/チャコール, ガッシュ/54×72 cm

The Kids / 1981 / Charcoal, gouache / 14″×17″
子供達/1981/チャコール, ガッシュ/42×51 cm

95

CATHY BARANCIK キャシー・バランシック

Her colors are as beautiful as butterfly's. They are combined with the warmth in her pastel drawings, which are brimming with charm and daintiness. (Pater Sato)
虹のような色彩の美しさ。パステル画の温もりとあいまって，甘さとやさしさが溢れる。(ペーター佐藤)

TITLE **Margaret In Blue Dress** / Unpublished / 1982 / Pastel / 8″×12″
青いドレスのマーガレット/未発表作品/1982/パステル/24×36cm

TITLE **Spring Fashion** / CLIENT Minneapolis Star & Tribune / Unpublished / 1984 / MEDIA Pastel / 7″×10″
スプリングファッション／未発表作品／1984／パステル／21×30cm

TITLE **Woman At Mirror** / CLIENT Vogue Magazine / Unpublished / 1984 / MEDIA Pastel / 17″×17″
鏡を見る女／未発表作品／1984／パステル／51×51cm

TITLE CLIENT MEDIA
Active Sportswear / Minneapolis Star & Tribune / Unpublished / 1984 / Pastel / 18″×24″
アクティブ・スポーツウェア／未発表作品／1984／パステル／54×72cm

TITLE MEDIA
Dinner In New York / Unpublished / 1983 / Pastel / 15″×20″
ニューヨークのディナー／未発表作品／1983／パステル／45×60cm

Cathy Barancik

TITLE   CLIENT   MEDIA
Blue Chemise / Vogue Patterns / Magazine / 1984 / Pastel / 10″×15″
ブルー・シュミーズ／雑誌／1984／パステル／30×45cm

TITLE   CLIENT   MEDIA
Chemise / Vogue Patterns / Magazine / 1984 / Pastel / 10″×15″
シュミーズ／雑誌／1984／パステル／30×45cm

Style Poster / Minneapolis Star & Tribune / 1984 / Pastel / 18″×24″

スタイル・ポスター/1984/パステル/54×72cm

Fall Accessories / Bergdorf Goodman / Instore Poster / 1983 / Pastel / 17″×17″

秋のアクセサリー/店内ポスター/1983/パステル/51×51cm

Delman Shoes / Bergdorf Goodman / Instore Poster / 1983 / Pastel / 17″×17″
デルマン・シューズ//店内ポスター/1983//パステル/51×51cm

TITLE
Woman In Hat / Unpublished / 1984 / Pastel / 18″×24″
帽子をかぶった女/未発表作品/1984/パステル/54×72cm

TITLE
Delman Shoes / Bergdorf Goodman / Instore Poster / 1983 / Pastel / 17″×17″
デルマン・シューズ/店内ポスター/パステル/1983/51×51cm

BOB HIEMSTRA ボブ・ヒムストラ

Bob Hiemstra's refinement charm and city sophistication can be seen in his simple black and white drawings. (Pater Sato)
洗練，甘さ，そして都会的なデリケートさ。黒と白のシンプルな作品に本領が見える。（ペーター 佐藤）

Sun Glasses / Artist's Portfolio / Pastel / 8″×13″
サングラス/ポートフォリオ/パステル/24×39cm

TITLE **Blue Blazer** / CLIENT Barney's / MEDIA N.Y. Times, Wall Street Journal / Pastel / 8″×10″
ブルーのブレザー/雑誌/パステル/24×30cm

TITLE **Suede Coat** / CLIENT Peter Rogers Assoc. / MEDIA W.W.D. / Pastel / 11″×14″
スウェードのコート/新聞/パステル/33×42cm

TITLE
Trench Dress / Henri Bendel / W. / Pastel / 14″×18″
トレンチ・ドレス/新聞/パステル/42×54cm

TITLE
Stephen Sprouse Bathing Suit / Henri Bendel / N.Y. Times / Pastel / 4″×6″
水着/雑誌/パステル/12×18cm

HIEMSTRA

HIEMSTRA

Pin Stripe Suit / Barney's / N.Y. Times, Wall Street Journal / Pastel / 8″ ×10″
ピンストライプのスーツ/雑誌/パステル/24×30 cm

Artists' Profile

ANTONIO LOPEZ アントニオ・ロペス

Place of Birth: Utuado, Puerto Rico

QUESTIONS

1. Who or what has most influenced your artistic style?
MUSIC + DANCE, PEOPLE

2. Do you work from real life models or photographs for your drawings?
MODELS.

3. How do you keep up with fashion information and trends?
TRAVELING.

4. Who is your favorite fashion designer?
I HAVE MANY.

5. Who is your favorite fashion photographer?
HELMUT NEWTON - EVERY 6 MONTHS A NEW ONE.

6. Who is your favorite artist (painter, sculptor, etc.)?
PICASSO.

7. What is your favorite fashion magazine?
AMERICAN VOGUE.

8. Who do you feel projects your ideal female image?
PALOMA PICASSO

9. Who do you feel projects your ideal male image?
TARZAN

10. Please describe your own favorite personal clothing style.
EDWARDIAN

11. What is your favorite two-color combination?
PURPLE + BLUE

12. What is your favorite kind of music?
AFRO-CUBAN

13. What do you feel is the most fashionable place in New York?
MR. CHOW

14. Describe in three sentences about New York's charm for you.
IT'S MODERN, EVERYONE IS HERE OR COMES HERE - AND IT'S OPEN 24 HOURS A DAY.

15. What kind of artistic qualities are you attempting to capture in drawing?
ELEGANCE - STYLE - DRAMA

16. What changes do you foresee in fashion 10 years later?
MORE ETHNIC INFLUENCES,

1. アートスタイルで影響を受けている物、或いは人物を答えてください。
音楽、ダンス、人々。

2. 作品を描くときはモデルを使いますか、写真を使いますか？
モデル。

3. ファッションの情報や傾向を何から得ようとしていますか？
旅行。

4. 好きなファッションデザイナーは？
たくさんいます。

5. 好きなファッションフォトグラファーは？
ヘルムート・ニュートンですが、半年毎に変わります。

6. 好きな芸術家（画家、彫刻家など）は？
ピカソ。

7. ファッション誌で気にいっているものは？
アメリカン・ヴォーグ。

8. "理想のイメージ"の女性は誰ですか？
パロマ・ピカソ。

9. "理想のイメージ"の男性は？
ターザン。

10. 自分が着る服はどういうスタイルが好ましいとお考えですか？
エドワード朝スタイル。

11. 2色の組み合わせで好きな配色を挙げてください。
パープルとブルー。

12. どんな音楽が好きですか？
アフロ・キューバン。

13. ニューヨークで最もファッショナブルな場所は？
ミスター・チャオ（レストラン）。

14. 3行でニューヨークの魅力を書いてください。
"現在"の街です。人々が集まる街です。24時間営業の街です。

15. 作品を描く際、どういう点を心がけていますか？
エレガンス——スタイル——ドラマ。

16. 10年後のファッションはどのように変化していると思いますか？
もっとエスニックになると思います。

JIM HOWARD ジム・ハワード

Date of Birth: 1930
Place of Birth: Texas

QUESTIONS

1. Who or what has most influenced your artistic style?
   ALL GREAT HUMANISTIC - REALISTIC ART - PAST - PRESENT

2. Do you work from real life models or photographs for your drawings?
   FROM PHOTOGRAPHS OF MY REAL LIFE MODELS

3. How do you keep up with fashion information and trends?
   WWD - EUROPEAN AND US FASHION MAGAZINES

4. Who is your favorite fashion designer?
   I HAVE NO SINGLE FAVORITE - EACH SEASON BRINGS NEW LIKES.

5. Who is your favorite fashion photographer?
   RICHARD AVEDON

6. Who is your favorite artist (painter, sculptor, etc.)?
   DEGAS

7. What is your favorite fashion magazine?
   LINEA ITALIAN

8. Who do you feel projects your ideal female image?
   GRETA GRETTA GARBO

9. Who do you feel projects your ideal male image?
   ROBERT TAYLOR

10. Please describe your own favorite personal clothing style.
    COSTUME - ECLECTIC (I'M PRESENTLY TRYING JAPANESE)

11. What is your favorite two-color combination?
    BLACK + TAUPE

12. What is your favorite kind of music?
    EARLY CLASSICAL - OPERA

13. What do you feel is the most fashionable place in New York?
    THE METROPOLITAN MUSEUM ON COSTUME INSTITUTE OPENING NIGHT

14. Describe in three sentences about New York's charm for you.
    FREEDOM OF EXPRESSION / MULTI CULTURE
    DIVERSITY OF LIFE STYLE

15. What kind of artistic qualities are you attempting to capture in drawing?
    HUMAN WARMTH WITH STRONG BASIC, CLASSIC DRAWING -
    WITH A THEATRICAL EDGE.

16. What changes do you foresee in fashion 10 years later?
    LESS NOSTALGIA
    CLEAN, EASY TO WEAR, MODERN, UNCLUTTERED
    HOPEFULLY BETTER CONSTRUCTION
    CLOTHES YOU DON'T NEED TO THINK ABOUT

1. アートスタイルで影響を受けている物、或いは人を答えてください。
古今東西の偉大な芸術作品、ヒューマンでリアリスティックな作品全てから影響を受けています。

2. 作品を描くときはモデルを使いますか、写真を使いますか？
マネキンの写真から。

3. ファッションの情報や傾向を何から得ようとしていますか？
W.W.D.紙、およびアメリカとヨーロッパで発行されているファッション雑誌。

4. 好きなファッションデザイナーは？
特定の人は挙げられません。シーズン毎に新しい人を好きになります。

5. 好きなファッションフォトグラファーは？
リチャード・アベドン。

6. 好きな芸術家（画家、彫刻家など）は？
ドガ。

7. ファッション誌で気にいっているものは？
リニア・モーダ。

8. "理想のイメージ"の女性は誰ですか？
グレタ・ガルボ。

9. "理想のイメージ"の男性は？
ロバート・テイラー。

10. 自分が着る服はどういうスタイルが好ましいとお考えですか？
エクレティックなコスチューム（今、ジャパニーズスタイルに挑戦しています）。

11. 2色の組み合わせで好きな配色を挙げてください。
黒と暗灰色。

12. どんな音楽が好きですか？
初期のクラシックな音楽——オペラなど。

13. ニューヨークで最もファッショナブルな場所は？
オープニングの夜のメトロポリタン・ミュージアム・コスチューム・インスティチュート。

14. 3行でニューヨークの魅力を書いてください。
表現の自由。種々の文化。様々なライフスタイル。

15. 作品を描く際、どういう点を心がけていますか？
確固としたベースに人間的な暖かみを持たせた、クラシックなドローイング。

16. 10年後のファッションはどのように変化していると思いますか？
ノスタルジックな要素は少なくなり、清潔さ、着やすさ、モダンですっきりした服が好まれるようになるでしょう。できれば良いカットの、着ていることを意識しないような服であってほしいですね。

PEDRO BARRIOS ペドロ・バリオス

Address: 359 W. 20th St., NY NY
Date of Birth: 1947
Place of Birth: Habana, Cuba

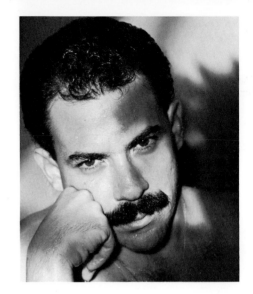

QUESTIONS

1. Who or what has most influenced your artistic style?
    Travelling

2. Do you work from real life models or photographs for your drawings?
    Anything, to capture the time, not the moment

3. How do you keep up with fashion information and trends?
    Lifestyle dictates fashion

4. Who is your favorite fashion designer?
    Balenciaga

5. Who is your favorite fashion photographer?
    Munkacsi

6. Who is your favorite artist (painter, sculptor, etc.)?
    Picasso

7. What is your favorite fashion magazine?
    Vogue in the 1930's

8. Who do you feel projects your ideal female image?
    Audrey Hepburn

9. Who do you feel projects your ideal male image?
    Cary Grant

10. Please describe your own favorite personal clothing style.
    Classic, conservative & casual

11. What is your favorite two-color combination?
    Black & White

12. What is your favorite kind of music?
    Sambas & Bach

13. What do you feel is the most fashionable place in New York?
    Soho

14. Describe in three sentences about New York's charm for you.
    It's my hometown. the creative energy. It's melting pot quality.

15. What kind of artistic qualities are you attempting to capture in drawing?
    Abstracting the form into the simplest, flowing design

16. What changes do you foresee in fashion 10 years later?
    Nostalgia lovers will recycle the 80's. Classics will live forever!

1.アートスタイルで影響を受けている物，或いは人を答えてください。
旅行。

2.作品を描くときはモデルを使いますか，写真を使いますか？
瞬間ではなく，時を捉えることができるものなら何でも利用します。

3.ファッションの情報や傾向を何から得ようとしていますか？
ライフスタイルがファッションを決定します。

4.好きなファッションデザイナーは？
バレンシアーガ。

5.好きなファッションフォトグラファーは？
ムンカシ。

6.好きな芸術家（画家，彫刻家など）は？
ピカソ。

7.ファッション誌で気にいっているものは？
1930年代のヴォーグ。

8.″理想のイメージ″の女性は誰ですか？
オードリー・ヘップバーン。

9.″理想のイメージ″の男性は？
ケーリー・グラント。

10.自分が着る服はどういうスタイルが好ましいとお考えですか？
クラシック，コンサーバティブ，カジュアルがモットーです。

11.2色の組み合わせで好きな配色を挙げてください。
黒と白。

12.どんな音楽が好きですか？
サンバとバッハ。

13.ニューヨークで最もファッショナブルな場所は？
ソーホー地区。

14.3行でニューヨークの魅力を書いてください。
ここは私の街です。物を作り出すエネルギーを感じます。そうしたエネルギーが1つに溶けこんだ街です。

15.作品を描く際，どういう点を心がけていますか？
物の形をシンプルの極みに追いこみ，流れるようなデザインに抽象化することです。

16.10年後のファッションはどのように変化していると思いますか？
ノスタルジアは80年代に入って再び息を吹き返すでしょう。クラシックは永遠です！

J. CRAWFORD J.クロフォード

Date of Birth: 1930
Place of Birth: Jacksonville, Florida

QUESTIONS

1. Who or what has most influenced your artistic style?

   ?

2. Do you work from real life models or photographs for your drawings?

   MODELS & PHOTOS

3. How do you keep up with fashion information and trends?

   MAGAZINES

4. Who is your favorite fashion designer?

   CALVIN KLEIN

5. Who is your favorite fashion photographer?

   IRVING PENN

6. Who is your favorite artist (painter, sculptor, etc.)?

   DEGAS

7. What is your favorite fashion magazine?

   ENGLISH VOGUE & ELLE

8. Who do you feel projects your ideal female image?

   BROOKE SHEILDS

9. Who do you feel projects your ideal male image?

   JEFF ACQUILAN

10. Please describe your own favorite personal clothing style.

    TRADITIONAL

11. What is your favorite two-color combination?

    RED - BLACK

12. What is your favorite kind of music?

    ~~FAVORITE~~ *CLASSIC*

13. What do you feel is the most fashionable place in New York?

    GREOUILLE - ODEON -

14. Describe in three sentences about New York's charm for you.

    THE NEW ARCHITECTURE - OLD BUILDINGS - + THEATRE

15. What kind of artistic qualities are you attempting to capture in drawing?

    UNUSUAL POSES + MOOD

16. What changes do you foresee in fashion 10 years later?

    RETURN TO ARTWORK

WILLIAM RIESER ウィリアム・リーサー

Address: *c/o Michele Sannders, 309 W. 76th St., NY NY*
Date of Birth: 1954
Place of Birth: Madison, Wisconsin

QUESTIONS

1. Who or what, has most influenced your artistic style? *I would have to say that going back to the beginning Marvel comic books influenced my style and interest in art. esp spiderman.*

2. Do you work from real life models or photographs for your drawings? *Mostly Photo's*

3. How do you keep up with fashion information and trends? *With a combination of things. ▬▬ - ▬▬ - Magazines, movies, plays, galleries and observation of people on the street.*

4. Who is your favorite fashion designer? *Giorgio Armani*

5. Who is your favorite fashion photographer? *Helmut Newton*

6. Who is your favorite artist (painter, sculptor, etc.)? *Richard LINDNER*

7. What is your favorite fashion magazine? *DONNA*

8. Who do you feel projects your ideal female image? *MERYL STREEP*

9. Who do you feel projects your ideal male image? *CARY GRANT*

10. Please describe your own favorite personal clothing style. *I guess casual & comfortable would best describe it - Oversize sweaters and baggy pleated pants - tennis shoes.*

11. What is your favorite two-color combination? *Black/white*

12. What is your favorite kind of music? *Thats hard to say. I like a lot of diffent kinds of music depending on what I'm doing. Generally though I like more from the BEAT 3 TALKING HEADS*

13. What do you feel is the most fashionable place in New York? *ODEON*

14. Describe in three sentences about New York's charm for you. *I find N.Y. to be a place of incredible energy and excitement. There is a rawness and a sense of urgency to things, that doesn't exist anywhere else. I find that very inspirational and motivating.*

15. What kind of artistic qualities are you attempting to capture in drawing? *Action, movement and life. I want the work to have a sense of timing and moving through the line and color.*

16. What changes do you foresee in fashion 10 years later?

1.アートスタイルで影響を受けている物, 或いは人を答えてください。
ずいぶん昔の話になりますが, マーベル・コミックブックが私のスタイルに影響を与え, 絵画への関心をかきたててくれました。特にスパイダーマンです。

2.作品を描くときはモデルを使いますか, 写真を使いますか？
ほとんど写真からです。

3.ファッションの情報や傾向を何から得ようとしていますか？
雑誌, 映画, 演劇, ギャラリー, 通りを歩いている人々など様々なものから。

4.好きなファッションデザイナーは？
ジョルジュ・アルマーニ。

5.好きなファッションフォトグラファーは？
ヘルムート・ニュートン。

6.好きな芸術家（画家, 彫刻家など）は？
リチャード・リンドナー。

7.ファッション誌で気にいっているものは？
ドンナ。

8."理想のイメージ"の女性は誰ですか？
メリル・ストリープ。

9."理想のイメージ"の男性は？
ケーリー・グラント。

10.自分が着る服はどういうスタイルが好ましいとお考えですか？
カジュアルな着やすさというのが１番だと思います。大きなセーターとプリーツの大きなズボン, テニスシューズ。

11.2色の組み合わせで好きな配色を挙げてください。
黒と白。

12.どんな音楽が好きですか？
難しいですね──何をしているかによって好きな音楽がちがうのです。一般的にはビートの効いた音楽, トーキング・ヘッズなどが好きです。

13.ニューヨークで最もファッショナブルな場所は？
オデオン（レストラン）。

14.3行でニューヨークの魅力を書いてください。
ニューヨークはものすごいエネルギーを持つ刺激的な街です。むき出しのままの味と, 追いたてられるような感覚があります。こんな場所は他にはないでしょう。ひらめきと刺激の街ですね。

15.作品を描く際, どういう点を心がけていますか？
アクション, 動き, 生活。線と色で, 生きている, 動いているという感じを作品の中に表現したいと思います。

16.10年後のファッションはどのように変化していると思いますか？
？

DAVID CROLAND デビッド・クローランド

Place of Birth: New York

Photo: Tim Sheaffer

QUESTIONS

1.   Who or what has most influenced your artistic style?   *MY MOTHER*

2.   Do you work from real life models or photographs for your drawings?   *BOTH*

3.   How do you keep up with fashion information and trends?   *OPEN EYES*

4.   Who is your favorite fashion designer?   *Y.SL.*

5.   Who is your favorite fashion photographer?   *AVEDON*

6.   Who is your favorite artist (painter, sculptor, etc.)?   *ARP, MIRO, PICASSO.*

7.   What is your favorite fashion magazine?   *AMERICAN VOGUE*

8.   Who do you feel projects your ideal female image?   *ME*

9.   Who do you feel projects your ideal male image?   *ME*

10.   Please describe your own favorite personal clothing style.   *RELAXING FORMAL*

11.   What is your favorite two-color combination?   *WHITE-NAVY*

12.   What is your favorite kind of music?   *MOOD MUSIC*

13.   What do you feel is the most fashionable place in New York?   *MY APARTMENT*

14.   Describe in three sentences about New York's charm for you.   *PEOPLE, PLACES, THINGS.*

15.   What kind of artistic qualities are you attempting to capture in drawing?   *GOOD ONES.*

16.   What changes do you foresee in fashion 10 years later?   *THE REVERSE OF WHATS HAPPENING TODAY.*

1．アートスタイルで影響を受けている物，或いは人物を答えてください。
私の母。

2．作品を描くときはモデルを使いますか，写真を使いますか？
両方。

3．ファッションの情報や傾向を何から得ようとしていますか？
目を開けていること。

4．好きなファッションデザイナーは？
イヴ・サン・ローラン。

5．好きなファッションフォトグラファーは？
アベドン。

6．好きな芸術家（画家，彫刻家など）は？
ミロ，ピカソ。

7．ファッション誌で気にいっているものは？
アープ，アメリカン・ヴォーグ。

8．"理想のイメージ"の女性は誰ですか？
私。

9．"理想のイメージ"の男性は？
私。

10．自分が着る服はどういうスタイルが好ましいとお考えですか？
リラックスしたフォーマル。

11．2色の組み合わせで好きな配色を挙げてください。
白とネイビーブルー。

12．どんな音楽が好きですか？
ムードミュージック。

13．ニューヨークで最もファッショナブルな場所は？
私のアパート。

14．3行でニューヨークの魅力を書いてください。
人，場所，物。

15．作品を描く際，どういう点を心がけていますか？
良い作品。

16．10年後のファッションはどのように変化していると思いますか？
今日起こっていることの全く反対のこと。

GEORGE STAVRINOS ジョージ・スタヴリノス

Address: 76 W. 86th St., NY 10024
Date of Birth: 1948
Place of Birth: Boston, Massachusetts

QUESTIONS

1. Who or what has most influenced your artistic style? THE AMERICAN ILLUSTRATORS OF THE EARLY TO MID 20TH CENTURY SUCH AS PARRISH, LEYENDECKER, ROCKWELL AND THE FILMS OF ALFRED HITCHCOCK.

2. Do you work from real life models or photographs for your drawings? I WORK FROM POLAROID PHOTOS THAT I TAKE OF MODELS — USUALLY FRIENDS— WHO POSE WEARING THE CLOTHING I AM TO ILLUSTRATE. I USE NATURAL LIGHT COMBINED WITH DRAMATIC ARTIFICIAL LIGHT AND FLASH.

3. How do you keep up with fashion information and trends? THROUGH FASHION MAGAZINES + NEWSPAPERS (AMERICAN AND EUROPEAN)

4. Who is your favorite fashion designer? THE DESIGNS OF PERRY ELLIS, KRIZIA, BEENE, ARMANI AND MIYAKE ARE THE ONES I HAVE ENJOYED ILLUSTRATING THE MOST

5. Who is your favorite fashion photographer? BRUCE WEBBER, NORMAN PARKINSON

6. Who is your favorite artist (painter, sculptor, etc.)? JOHN SINGER SARGENT, CARAVAGGIO, INGRES

7. What is your favorite fashion magazine? L'UOMO VOGUE

8. Who do you feel projects your ideal female image? DANTE GABRIEL ROSSETTI (PRE-RAPHAELITE PAINTERS) JESSICA LANGE, INGRID BERGMAN (ACTRESSES)

9. Who do you feel projects your ideal male image? J.C. LEYENDECKER (ILLUSTRATOR) GARY COOPER (ACTOR)

10. Please describe your own favorite personal clothing style. SIMPLE, COMFORTABLE, CLASSIC, NEUTRAL TONES, NATURAL WEAVES

11. What is your favorite two-color combination? BLACK + BLUE

12. What is your favorite kind of music? JAZZ, ITALIAN OPERA AND COLE PORTER

13. What do you feel is the most fashionable place in New York? THREE LIVES BOOKSTORE AND TEXARKANA RESTAURANT

14. Describe in three sentences about New York's charm for you. FOR ME, THE CHARM OF NEW YORK RESULTS FROM THE MIXTURE OF PEOPLES WHO INHABIT THE CITY — WHOSE CULTURAL BACKGROUNDS, MUSIC AND LANGUAGE BLEND TO GIVE NEW YORK IT'S HEARTBEAT. THIS UNIQUE MIXTURE IS WHAT MAKES NEW YORK CITY THE EXCITING PLACE THAT IT IS.

15. What kind of artistic qualities are you attempting to capture in drawing? STRONG, GRAPHIC LAYOUTS; SENSUAL, REALISTIC SURFACES AND TEXTURES THAT MAKE THE VIEWER WANT TO REACH OUT AND TOUCH IT.

16. What changes do you foresee in fashion 10 years later? IN 10 YEARS, FASHION WILL PROBABLY RETURN ONCE AGAIN TO SIMPLE, VERSATILE, CLASSIC DESIGNS AFTER GOING THROUGH FADS, AND EXTREME, TEMPORARY DESIGNS THAT WON'T HAVE MUCH LASTING POWER.

1．アートスタイルで影響を受けている物，或いは人を答えてください。
20世紀初頭から中期にかけて活躍したアメリカのイラストレーター達。パリッシュ、レイエンデッカー、ロックウェルなど。アルフレッド・ヒッチコックの映画。

2．作品を描くときはモデルを使いますか、写真を使いますか？
モデル——大概は友人ですが——に描きたい服を着てもらい、それをポラロイド写真で撮影してから作品にとりかかります。ドラマティックな人工の光と影を自然光と組み合わせて描きます。

3．ファッションの情報や傾向を何から得ようとしていますか？
ファッション誌や新聞から（アメリカやヨーロッパのもの）。

4．好きなファッションデザイナーは？
ペリー・エリス、クリツィア、ジェフェリー・ビーン、ジョルジュ・アルマーニ、イッセイ・ミヤケのデザインは本当に楽しんで描きました。

5．好きなファッションフォトグラファーは？
ブルース・ウェバー、ノーマン・パーキンソン。

6．好きな芸術家（画家，彫刻家など）は？
ジョン・シンガー・サージェント、カラバジオ、イングレス。

7．ファッション誌で気にいっているものは？
ルオモ・ヴォーグ。

8．"理想のイメージ"の女性は誰ですか？
ダンテ、ガブリエル、ロセッティ（ラファエル以前の画家達）が描く女性。ジェシカ・ラング、イングリッド・バーグマン（女優）。

9．"理想のイメージ"の男性は？
J．C．レイエンデッカー（イラストレーター）とゲーリー・クーパー（男優）。

10．自分が着る服はどういうスタイルが好ましいとお考えですか？
シンプルで着やすく、クラシックな雰囲気。中間色で自然な織りの服。

11．2色の組み合わせで好きな配色を挙げてください。
黒と青。

12．どんな音楽が好きですか？
ジャズ、イタリアのオペラ、コール・ポーター。

13．ニューヨークで最もファッショナブルな場所は？
3軒の大きな本屋とテキサカナ・レストラン。

14．3行でニューヨークの魅力を書いてください。
ニューヨークの魅力は、異なる文化的背景、音楽、言語を持つ様々な国籍の人々がここに集まってきている点だと思います。この異質のものがぶつかりあうところに現在のニューヨークの活気があるのではないでしょうか。

15．作品を描く際、どういう点を心がけていますか？
強く、グラフィックなレイアウト。見る人が手を伸ばして触れたくなるほどに官能的でリアリスティックな面、質感。

16．10年後のファッションはどのように変化していると思いますか？
この10年間でファッションはその場だけで長く生き残りそうもない過度のデザインを経て、再びシンプルで何にでも合わせられるクラシックなものへと戻っていくでしょう。

KICHISABURO OGAWA キチサブロー・オガワ

Address: 1450 2nd Ave., NY NY
Date of Birth: 1946
Place of Birth: Japan

QUESTIONS

1. Who or what has most influenced your artistic style?
   The ART DECO PERIOD, LEPAPE, BENITO

2. Do you work from real life models or photographs for your drawings?
   mostly from photographs, sometimes models,

3. How do you keep up with fashion information and trends?
   Mostly through the media - newspaper & magazines. I pay attention to what is in happening current trends-especially music

4. Who is your favorite fashion designer?
   SONIA RYKIEL

5. Who is your favorite fashion photographer?
   Helmet Newton.

6. Who is your favorite artist (painter, sculptor, etc.)?
   MATISE

7. What is your favorite fashion magazine?
   PARIS Vogue.

8. Who do you feel projects your ideal female image?
   FROM G. Hommel's photo, Louise Brooks

9. Who do you feel projects your ideal male image?

10. Please describe your own favorite personal clothing style.
    Casual. Easy looking. sportswear style

11. What is your favorite two-color combination?
    Black / RED

12. What is your favorite kind of music?
    I enjoy all kinds of music

13. What do you feel is the most fashionable place in New York?
    I find fashion and style all over the city. There is not any one place for it as far as I concerned. It is in the streets more than anywhere else

14. Describe in three sentences about New York's charm for you.
    NY has always enormous amount of energy and individuality for me. If there is something new and creative happning in the world chances you'll find it in this city and Tokyo now. The variety of people are always help to keep me feeling alive and excited about living here

15. What kind of artistic qualities are you attempting to capture in drawing?
    Basically a clean. simple but highly stylized kind of drawing.

16. What changes do you foresee in fashion 10 years later?
    I see Haute Couture becoming even less influential than it is already. Style will probably continue to stay on the casual side with little changes from season to season to help keep people interested but on the whole I think the sportswear influence will remain storng.

1. アートスタイルで影響を受けている物、或いは人を答えてください。
   アール・デコ時代、レペペ、ベニト。

2. 作品を描くときはモデルを使いますか、写真を使いますか？
   大概は写真からですが、モデルも時々使います。

3. ファッションの情報や傾向を何から得ようとしていますか？
   ほとんど新聞や雑誌といったメディアからです。今、何が起こっているか、特に音楽の流行については注意しています。

4. 好きなファッションデザイナーは？
   ソニア・リキエル。

5. 好きなファッションフォトグラファーは？
   ヘルムート・ニュートン。

6. 好きな芸術家（画家、彫刻家など）は？
   マチス。

7. ファッション誌で気にいっているものは？
   パリ・ヴォーグ。

8. "理想のイメージ"の女性は誰ですか？
   G・ホメルの写真。ルイーズ・ブルックス。

9. "理想のイメージ"の男性は？
   ？

10. 自分が着る服はどういうスタイルが好ましいとお考えですか？
    カジュアル。着やすそうなスポーツウェアスタイル。

11. 2色の組み合わせで好きな配色を挙げてください。
    黒と赤。

12. どんな音楽が好きですか？
    音楽なら何でも好きです。

13. ニューヨークで最もファッショナブルな場所は？
    ファッショナブルでスタイルを持った場所は街中にあります。1ヶ所には限定できないと思います。ニューヨークの通りこそ、最もファッショナブルな場所です。

14. 3行でニューヨークの魅力を書いてください。
    私にとってニューヨークはものすごいエネルギーと個性の街です。何か新しいこと、何かクリエイティブなことが世界のどこかで起こったとすれば、すぐにニューヨークと東京で発表されます。様々な人々が私に刺激を与え、生きることの素晴しさを教えてくれます。

15. 作品を描く際、どういう点を心がけていますか？
    基本的には清潔感があって、シンプルで、しかも洗練されたスタイルを持つ
    つドローイングを心がけています。

16. 10年後のファッションはどのように変化していると思いますか？
    オートクチュールの影響力は少なくなり、季節に影響されることのないカジュアルなスタイルが人々に愛されていくでしょう。全体的にはスポーツウェアの影響が強く残ると思います。

MICHAEL VAN HORN マイケル・ヴァン・ホーン

Address: c/o Tom Booth, 425 W. 23rd St., NY NY 10011
Place of Birth: Florida

QUESTIONS

1. Who or what has most influenced your artistic style? Ingres, Schiele, Vargas, Antonio Lopez, Tamara De Lempika

2. Do you work from real life models or photographs for your drawings? Both

3. How do you keep up with fashion information and trends? trips to Paris, publications, fashion shows

4. Who is your favorite fashion designer? Adrian

5. Who is your favorite fashion photographer? Cecil Beaton

6. Who is your favorite artist (painter, sculptor, etc.)? Velázquez Clyfford Still, Brancusi

7. What is your favorite fashion magazine? I buy them all

8. Who do you feel projects your ideal female image? Irene Castle

9. Who do you feel projects your ideal male image? Frank O'hara

10. Please describe your own favorite personal clothing style. I always liked the Gene Kelly look

11. What is your favorite two-color combination?

12. What is your favorite kind of music?

13. What do you feel is the most fashionable place in New York? My apartment

14. Describe in three sentences about New York's charm for you. I don't think of New York as charming. It's certainly not that. It's the one city in America that has the best and worst of everything.

15. What kind of artistic qualities are you attempting to capture in drawing? Exageration without being obvious and well planned composition.

16. What changes do you foresee in fashion 10 years later? I don't know but I can't wait to see. maybe less emphasis on style but more on technique

1.アートスタイルで影響を受けている物、或いは人を答えてください。
ヴァルガス、アントニオ・ロペス、タマラ・デ・レンピカ。

2.作品を描くときはモデルを使いますか？写真を使いますか？
両方。

3.ファッションの情報や傾向を何から得ようとしていますか？
パリへの旅行、出版物、ファッション・ショー。

4.好きなファッションデザイナーは？
エイドリアン。

5.好きなファッションフォトグラファーは？
セシル・ビートン。

6.好きな芸術家（画家、彫刻家など）は？
ヴェラスケス、クリフォード・スティル、ブランクーシ。

7.ファッション誌で気にいっているものは？
全部買っています。

8."理想のイメージ"の女性は誰ですか？
イレーネ・カスル。

9."理想のイメージ"の男性は？
フランク・オハラ。

10.自分が着る服はどういうスタイルが好ましいとお考えですか？
ジーン・ケリーのスタイルが好きです。

11.2色の組み合わせで好きな配色を挙げてください。
？

12.どんな音楽が好きですか。
？

13.ニューヨークで最もファッショナブルな場所は？
私のアパート。

14.3行でニューヨークの魅力を書いてください。
ニューヨークがチャーミングだとはとても思えません。何に関してもベストと
ワーストの両方を持っている唯一の街だという気がします。

15.作品を描く際、どういう点を心がけていますか？
さりげない誇張とよく練られた構成。

16.10年後のファッションはどのように変化していると思いますか？
どうなるかわかりませんが、早く見たいですね。多分スタイルをあまり強く
打ち出さないで技術に重点が置かれるのでは？

MARTIN HOFFMAN マーティン・ホフマン

Address: Box 50, RD2, Worcester NY 12197
Date of Birth: 1935
Place of Birth: St. Augustine, Florida

QUESTIONS

1. Who or what has most influenced your artistic style?
   Botticelli's drawings — + Patriarch Hui-Neng (first great Zen Master)

2. Do you work from real life models or photographs for your drawings?
   sometimes both but mostly from imagination.

3. How do you keep up with fashion information and trends?
   travel + read + people watch

4. Who is your favorite fashion designer?
   no favorite { for advertising - Ralph Lauren / for fit - Calvin Klein / for fabric - Armani

5. Who is your favorite fashion photographer?
   no favorite { Helmut Newton -settings- / Guy Bourdin - models -

6. Who is your favorite artist (painter, sculptor, etc.)?
   Fra Angelico - Brancusi -

7. What is your favorite fashion magazine?
   ~~no favorite~~ *(American) Vogue*

8. Who do you feel projects your ideal female image?
   An annonymous woman of great physical beauty + intelligence who keeps a low profile + serene dignity.

9. Who do you feel projects your ideal male image?
   a dashing gentleman accomplished in manners of taste who is skilled above all in the perception of beauty + shuns notoriety

10. Please describe your own favorite personal clothing style.
    The Classics in soft bulky fabrics + natural colors

11. What is your favorite two-color combination?
    Ivory + gray

12. What is your favorite kind of music?
    (Chopin nocturns) - Erik Satie - (Nigerian Ju-Ju) (Jamaican Dub)

13. What do you feel is the most fashionable place in New York? *in the World?*
    — Secret meetings at the Waldorf Astoria — Brasserie Lipp in Paris (1st floor Banketto)

14. Describe in three sentences about New York's charm for you.
    Long Walks in November - Exploring Museums + galleries - discovering new Restaurants' in the Village — watching the input of fresh talent in Soho

15. What kind of artistic qualities are you attempting to capture in drawing?
    Spontaniety - profundity - participation + warmth - humor

16. What changes do you foresee in fashion 10 years later?
    Fashion will disappear for those who master it.

1.アートスタイルで影響を受けている物，或いは人物を答えてください。
　ボッティチェリの絵。Hui-Neng 先生（偉大な禅の導師）。

2.作品を描くときはモデルを使いますか，写真を使いますか？
　両方使うこともありますが，大概はイマジネーションからです。

3.ファッションの情報や傾向を何から得ようとしていますか？
　旅行，読書，人々を観察することから。

4.好きなファッションデザイナーは？
　好みなし。広告ではラルフ・ローレン，着やすさではカルバン・クライン，ファブリックではジョルジュ・アルマーニ。

5.好きなファッションフォトグラファーは？
　好みなし。セッティングのうまさはヘルムート・ニュートン，モデルの使い方はギー・ブーディン。

6.好きな芸術家（画家，彫刻家など）は？
　フラ・アンジェリコ。ブランクーシ。

7.ファッション誌で気にいっているものは？
　アメリカン・ヴォーグ。

8."理想のイメージ"の女性は誰ですか？
　出しゃばらず，静かな気品を持ち，美しい肉体と知性を兼ね備えた女性。

9."理想のイメージ"の男性は？
　趣味の良い前向きな男性。特に美しいものを理解し，悪評を避けることをわきまえた人。

10.自分が着る服はどういうスタイルが好ましいとお考えですか？
　やわらかでゆったりした生地，ナチュラルな色のクラシックなスタイル。

11.2色の組み合わせで好きな配色を挙げてください。
　アイボリーとグレイ。

12.どんな音楽が好きですか？
　ショパンのノクターン。エリック・サティ。ナイジェリアのジュージュー。ジャマイカのダブ。

13.ニューヨークで最もファッショナブルな場所は？
　ウォルドーフ・アストリアホテルでの密会。世界中でという意味なら，パリのブラセリエ・リップ（1Fのバンケットルーム）。

14.3行でニューヨークの魅力を書いてください。
　11月の長い散歩――美術館やギャラリーを見て歩くこと――グリニッジヴィレッジの新しいレストランを発見すること――ソーホーで新しい才能の芽ばえを見守ること。

15.作品を描く際，どういう点を心がけていますか？
　自然さ――深味――気持ちをこめること――暖かさ――ユーモア。

16.10年後のファッションはどのように変化していると思いますか？
　ファッションを自分のものにしてしまった人には，もはや存在しないものとなっているでしょう。

HARVEY BOYD ハービー・ボイド

Date of Birth: 1941
Place of Birth: Hartford, Connecticut

QUESTIONS

1. Who or what has most influenced your artistic style?
   ~~MY ART~~ I DON'T KNOW ABOUT MOST BUT ANXIETY HAS A LOT TO DO WITH IT.

2. Do you work from real life models or photographs for your drawings?
   BOTH — PLUS FROM MY IMAGINATION

3. How do you keep up with fashion information and trends?
   KEEP YOUR EYES, NOSE, AND OTHER SENSES SHARP STAY CURIOUS

4. Who is your favorite fashion designer? I'M A FAN OF MANY DESIGNERS — YSL · WILLI SMITH · FERNANDO SANCHEZ · REI KAWAKUBO · BEENE · ARMANI · BETSEY JOHNSON

5. Who is your favorite fashion photographer? A~O OR ANDON
   DON'T HAVE ONE

6. Who is your favorite artist (painter, sculptor, etc.)?
   INFLUENCED BY MANY ~ KNOWN AND UNKNOWN

7. What is your favorite fashion magazine?
   NO FAVORITE - READ THEM ALL

8. Who do you feel projects your ideal female image?
   SOMEWHERE BETWEEN GRACE JONES MERYL STREEP DORIS LESSING TONI MORRISON + BOY GEORGE

9. Who do you feel projects your ideal male image? TONI
   SOMEWHERE BETWEEN MICHAEL JACKSON — MALCOLM X MICK JAGGER · MYRON COHEN · AL GREEN AND PUSHKIN PLUS JAMES DAVIS AND HERT

10. Please describe your own favorite personal clothing style.
    COMFORTABLE

11. What is your favorite two-color combination?
    MOST ANY TWO COLORS LOOK WELL TOGETHER TO ME

12. What is your favorite kind of music?
    NO FAVORITE — BUT I LIKE "JUJU" MUSIC A LOT RIGHT NOW

13. What do you feel is the most fashionable place in New York?
    WHEREVER YOU'RE HAVING A GOOD TIME AT THE MOMENT

14. Describe in three sentences about New York's charm for you.
    IN ONE WORD — DIVERSITY

15. What kind of artistic qualities are you attempting to capture in drawing?
    I'LL HAVE TO THINK ABOUT THAT

16. What changes do you foresee in fashion 10 years later?
    DEPENDS MOSTLY ON WHAT IDEAS COME FROM WOMEN

1．アートスタイルで影響を受けている物，或いは人を答えてください。
1番と言われるとよくわかりませんが，不安や懸念からは大きな影響を受けていると思います。

2．作品を描くときはモデルを作りますか，写真を使いますか？
両方です——それに加えて私のイマジネーションからです。

3．ファッションの情報や傾向を何から得ようとしていますか？
目を配り，鼻をきかせ，感覚を総動員させ続けること，あらゆるものに興味を持つこと。

4．好きなファッションデザイナーは？
好きなデザイナーがたくさんいます——イヴ・サン・ローラン，ウィリー・スミス，フェルナンド・サンチェス，川久保玲，ジェフェリー・ビーン，ジョルジュ・アルマーニ，ベッツィ・ジョンソン，など，など，など。

5．好きなファッションフォトグラファーは？
いません。

6．好きな芸術家（画家，彫刻家など）は？
有名，無名に関わらず，あらゆる芸術家に影響されてきました。

7．ファッション誌で気にいっているものは？
好きなのはありません——全部読みます。

8．"理想のイメージ"の女性は誰ですか？
グレース・ジョーンズ，メリル・ストリープ，ドリス・レッシング，トニ・モリソン，それにボーイ・ジョージといったところです。

9．"理想のイメージ"の男性は？
マイケル・ジャクソン，マルカム・X，ミック・ジャガー，マイロン・コーヘン，アル・グリーン，プッシュキンプラスジェームス・ディビス・ヘリーといったところです。

10．自分が着る服はどういうスタイルが好ましいとおconsidえですか？
着やすさ。

11．2色の組み合わせで好きな配色を挙げてください。
どんな組み合わせでも美しいと思います。

12．どんな音楽が好きですか？
特に好みはありませんが，今はジュージューが好きです。

13．ニューヨークで最もファッショナブルな場所は？
その瞬間に楽しくすごせる場所なら，どこでもファッショナブルだと思います。

14．3行でニューヨークの魅力を書いてください。
一言で言えば，多様性でしょうか。

15．作品を描く際，どういう点を心がけていますか？
それについてはよく考えなければなりません。

16．10年後のファッションはどのように変化していると思いますか？
女性から生まれるアイディアがどんなものであるかによって，ちがってきます。

MATS GUSTAVSON マッツ・グスタブソン

Address: c/o Tom Booth, 425 W. 23rd St., NY NY 10011
Date of Birth: 1951
Place of Birth: Sweden

QUESTIONS

1.   Who or what has most influenced your artistic style?
ANYTHING THAT GOES ON AT THE MOMENT — THE SENSE OF "NOW"

2.   Do you work from real life models or photographs for your drawings?
I WORK FROM MODELS, FROM POLAROIDS OR FROM JUST A CONCEPT

3.   How do you keep up with fashion information and trends?
I TRY TO TRAVEL A LOT. THE BEST INFORMATION I GET FROM "THE STREET".

4.   Who is your favorite fashion designer?
COCO CHANEL

5.   Who is your favorite fashion photographer?
MAN RAY (IF YOU CAN CALL HIM A FASHION PHOTOGRAPHER — — HE SURE WAS FASHIONABLE)

6.   Who is your favorite artist (painter, sculptor, etc.)?
THERE ARE MANY — HENRI MATISSE IS ONE

7.   What is your favorite fashion magazine?
I DON'T HAVE ANY

8.)   Who do you feel projects your ideal female image?
IT'S VERY LIMITING TO HAVE IDEAL IMAGES, I THINK

9.)   Who do you feel projects your ideal male image?

10.   Please describe your own favorite personal clothing style.
UNCONVENTIONALLY CONSERVATIVE

11.   What is your favorite two-color combination?
BLACK / WHITE

12.   What is your favorite kind of music?
IT DEPENDS ON THE SITUATION AND WHAT MOOD I'M IN.

13.   What do you feel is the most fashionable place in New York?
THE STREETS

14.   Describe in three sentences about New York's charm for you.
THE (MIX OF) PEOPLE THE ENERGY THE TOLERANCE

15.   What kind of artistic qualities are you attempting to capture in drawing?
SIMPLICITY BEAUTY HUMOR

16.   What changes do you foresee in fashion 10 years later?
FASHION WILL CONCERN A LOT MORE PEOPLE EAST MEETS WEST " IS ALREADY A FACT. AND THE WORLD KEEPS ON TURNING.

1 . アートスタイルで影響を受けている物, 或いは人を答えてください。
　その瞬間に起こるすべてのこと——"今"という感覚。

2 . 作品を描くときはモデルを使いますか, 写真を使いますか？
　モデルかポラロイド写真。ただコンセプトだけで描くこともあります。

3 . ファッションの情報や傾向を何から得ようとしていますか？
　なるべく旅をしようと心がけています。1番の情報は街から得られます。

4 . 好きなファッションデザイナーは？
　ココ・シャネル。

5 . 好きなファッションフォトグラファーは？
　マン・レイ。

6 . 好きな芸術家（画家,彫刻家など）は？
　たくさんいます。アンリ・マティスもそのうちの1人です。

7 . ファッション誌で気にいっているものは？
　特にありません。

8 . "理想のイメージ"の女性は誰ですか？
　理想像を持つのは自分を限定することになると思います。

9 . "理想のイメージ"の男性は？
　同上。

10 . 自分が着る服はどういうスタイルが好ましいとお考えですか？
　きゅうくつでないコンサーバティブ。

11 . 2色の組み合わせで好きな配色を挙げてください。
　黒と白。

12 . どんな音楽が好きですか。
　その時の状態と気分によってちがいます。

13 . ニューヨークで最もファッショナブルな場所は？
　街。

14 . 3行でニューヨークの魅力を書いてください。
　様々な人々。エネルギー。寛容さ。

15 . 作品を描く際, どういう点を心がけていますか？
　シンプル。美しさ。ユーモア。

16 . 10年後のファッションはどのように変化していると思いますか？
　もっと多くの人がファッションに関わってくるでしょう。"東西の出会い" は
　言うまでもありません。地球は回り続けるでしょう。

JOEL RESNICOFF ジョエル・レズニコフ

Address: 121 2nd Ave., #2 NY NY 10003
Date of Birth: 1948

QUESTIONS

1. Who or what has most influenced your artistic style?
EVERYTHING INFLUENCES ME

2. Do you work from real life models or photographs for your drawings?
FROM LIVE MODELS OR FROM MY IMAGINATION

3. How do you keep up with fashion information and trends?
I KEEP MY EYES & EARS OPEN.

4. Who is your favorite fashion designer?
I ADMIRE MANY DESIGNERS FOR DIFFERENT REASONS.

5. Who is your favorite fashion photographer?

6. Who is your favorite artist (painter, sculptor, etc.)?
MARK ROTHKO

7. What is your favorite fashion magazine?
I DO NOT HAVE A FAVORITE

8. Who do you feel projects your ideal female image?
IT IS VERY HARD FOR ANYONE HUMAN TO FIT MY IDEAL TYPE

9. Who do you feel projects your ideal male image?
SAME AS ABOVE

10. Please describe your own favorite personal clothing style.
BIG & COMFORTABLE

11. What is your favorite two-color combination?
CHARTRUSE & MAGENTA

12. What is your favorite kind of music?
DANCEABLE AND WITH SOUL

13. What do you feel is the most fashionable place in New York?
MANHATTAN

14. Describe in three sentences about New York's charm for you.
THE ENERGY. THE VARIETY. THE CREATIVITY

15. What kind of artistic qualities are you attempting to capture in drawing?
I WOULD LIKE FOR PEOPLE TO LOOK AT THE WORLD A LITTLE DIFFERENTLY AFTER LOOKING AT MY DRAWINGS

16. What changes do you foresee in fashion 10 years later?
PEOPLES ATTITUDES TOWARD FASHION WILL GO THROUGH RADICAL CHANGES — MORE BEAUTIFUL & RADIANT PEOPLE WILL EXIST.

1．アートスタイルで影響を受けている物，或いは人を答えてください。
全てが私に影響を与えます。

2．作品を描くときはモデルを作りますか，写真を使いますか？
モデル（マネキンではない）とイマジネーションから。

3．ファッションの情報や傾向を何から得ようとしていますか？
目と耳をいつもオープンにしています。

4．好きなファッションデザイナーは？
それぞれちがう理由でたくさんのデザイナーを尊敬しています。

5．好きなファッションフォトグラファーは？
？

6．好きな芸術家（画家，彫刻家など）は？
マーク・ロスコ。

7．ファッション誌で気にいっているものは？
特にありません。

8．"理想のイメージ"の女性は誰ですか？
理想にあてはまる人間を挙げるのは難しいですね。

9．"理想のイメージ"の男性は？
上に同じ。

10．自分が着る服はどういうスタイルが好ましいとお考えですか？
大きくて着やすい服。

11．2色の組み合わせで好きな配色を挙げてください。
シャトルース（ブルー系）とマジェンタ（ピンク系）。

12．どんな音楽が好きですか？
いい音楽で踊れるもの。

13．ニューヨークで最もファッショナブルな場所は？
マンハッタン。

14．3行でニューヨークの魅力を書いてください。
エネルギー，多様性，創造。

15．作品を描く際，どういう点を心がけていますか？
私の絵を見てから物の見方が少しがってきたと言われたい。

16．10年後のファッションはどのように変化していると思いますか？
ファッションに対する人々の態度は大きく変化するでしょう──もっと美しく，もっといきいきとした人々が生きているだろうと思います。

CATHY BARANCIK キャシー・バランシック

Date of Birth: 1954
Place of Birth: Hyland Park, Illinois

QUESTIONS

1. Who or what has most influenced your artistic style?

   Vertes

2. Do you work from real life models or photographs for your drawings?

   Real Life models

3. How do you keep up with fashion information and trends?

   Magazines, Streets,

4. Who is your favorite fashion designer?

   Yves StaanLaurent

5. Who is your favorite fashion photographer?

   Arthur Elgort

6. Who is your favorite artist (painter, sculptor, etc.)?

   Cy Twombly

7. What is your favorite fashion magazine?

   Vogue

8. Who do you feel projects your ideal female image?

   Meryl Streep

9. Who do you feel projects your ideal male image?

   Paul Newman

10. Please describe your own favorite personal clothing style.

    Agnes B

11. What is your favorite two-color combination?

    aqua & Lavender

12. What is your favorite kind of music?

    Motown

13. What do you feel is the most fashionable place in New York?

    Area

14. Describe in three sentences about New York's charm for you. *New Yorks charm and excitement for me lies in the fact that it is a complete city. Everything you could want is here and accessable.*

15. What kind of artistic qualities are you attempting to capture in drawing? *Expressionism through color & line*

16. What changes do you foresee in fashion 10 years later?

    I have no idea.

1．アートスタイルで影響を受けている物，或いは人を答えてください。
ベルテス。
2．作品を描くときはモデルを使いますか，写真を使いますか？
モデルから。
3．ファッションの情報や傾向を何から得ようとしていますか？
雑誌。ストリート。
4．好きなファッションデザイナーは？
イヴ・サン・ローラン。
5．好きなファッションフォトグラファーは？
アーサー・エルゴート。
6．好きな芸術家（画家，彫刻家など）は？
サイ・トウォンブリー。
7．ファッション誌で気にいっているものは？
ヴォーグ。
8．"理想のイメージ"の女性は誰ですか？
メリル・ストリープ。
9．"理想のイメージ"の男性は？
ポール・ニューマン。
10．自分が着る服はどういうスタイルが好ましいとお考えですか？
アグネス・Bの服。
11．2色の組み合わせで好きな配色を挙げてください。
水色とラベンダー。
12．どんな音楽が好きですか。
モータウンサウンド。
13．ニューヨークで最もファッショナブルな場所は？
エリア（ディスコクラブ）。
14．3行でニューヨークの魅力を書いてください。
完璧な街だから，魅力的で刺激的です。ほしい物はなんでもここにあり，手に入れることができるのです。
15．作品を描く際，どういう点を心がけていますか？
色と線を駆使した表現主義。
16．10年後のファッションはどのように変化していると思いますか？
わかりません。

BOB HIEMSTRA ボブ・ヒムストラ

Address: c/o Tom Booth, 425 W. 23rd St., NY NY 10011
Date of Birth: 1956
Place of Birth: U.S.A.

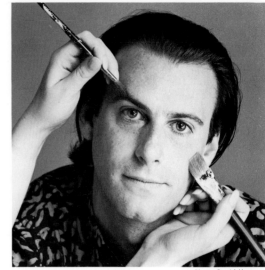

Photo: David Hartman

QUESTIONS

1. Who or what has most influenced your artistic style?

2. Do you work from real life models or photographs for your drawings?
   BOTH

3. How do you keep up with fashion information and trends?
   I speak to John Duka every morning

4. Who is your favorite fashion designer?
   KARL LAGERFELD

5. Who is your favorite fashion photographer?
   Barry Lategan

6. Who is your favorite artist (painter, sculptor, etc.)?
   Walter Keene

7. What is your favorite fashion magazine?
   Italian Bazaar

8. Who do you feel projects your ideal female image?

9. Who do you feel projects your ideal male image?

10. Please describe your own favorite personal clothing style.
    Classic — sort of ...

11. What is your favorite two-color combination?

12. What is your favorite kind of music?

13. What do you feel is the most fashionable place in New York?
    Madison Ave.

14. Describe in three sentences about New York's charm for you.

15. What kind of artistic qualities are you attempting to capture in drawing?

16. What changes do you foresee in fashion 10 years later?
    Wigs

1．アートスタイルで影響を受けている物，或いは人を答えてください。
　?
2．作品を描くときはモデルを使いますか，写真を使いますか？
　両方。
3．ファッションの情報や傾向を何から得ようとしていますか？
　毎朝，ジョン・デューカと話します。
4．好きなファッションデザイナーは？
　カール・ラガーフェルド。
5．好きなファッションフォトグラファーは？
　バーニー・ラティガン。
6．好きな芸術家（画家，彫刻家など）は？
　ウォルター・キーン。
7．ファッション誌で気にいっているものは？
　イタリアン・バザー。
8．"理想のイメージ"の女性は誰ですか？
　?
9．"理想のイメージ"の男性は？
　?
10．自分が着服はどういうスタイルが好ましいとお考えですか？
　ある種のクラシック。
11．2色の組み合わせで好きな配色を挙げてください。
　?
12．どんな音楽が好きですか？
　?
13．ニューヨークで最もファッショナブルな場所は？
　マディソン・アベニュー。
14．3行でニューヨークの魅力を書いてください。
　?
15．作品を描く際，どういう点を心がけていますか？
　?
16．10年後のファッションはどのように変化していると思いますか？
　かつら。

Afterword

As far as fashion illustration is concerned, it is agreed that style of fashion expression is always changing as well as fashion itself. Antonio Lopez once said, "I never create the same style."

His words might be considered the key basis of fashion illustration.

It was early in the 1970's when I first began to pay close attention to the job of a New York fashion illustrator. This was also when my interest in expression and style began to turn to fashion illustration.

In New York, which I have visited several times, I enjoyed reading and looking at the fashion section of the *New York Times*. In this section of the newspaper, I could see the fashion ads of every department store. To work for a New York department store as a fashion illustrator is a very prestigious position for a fashion illustrator.

A department store's ad such as Bonwit Teller or B. Altman enlarges the real world of style-drawings which have remained unchangeable since J. Crawford or Jim Howard in the 1950's. Bergdorf Goodman, which is regarded as a high-class department store, hired George Stavrinos who created his peculiar style of pencil-drawing after 1980. Macy's or Bloomingdale's enthusiastically employs young fresh artists. Through department store ads, I've come to know the world of fashion illustration and its trend in New York. The work of illustrators who were working for a fashion paper, *Woman's Wear Daily*, was also appealing to me. Antonio Lopez made his debut in this paper. I also first saw Joel Resnicoff's and Pedro Barrios's works in this paper. These two people are now working for Macy's. On the other hand, I fisrt observed work by David Croland or Mats Gustavson in *American Vogue* magazine.

The flow of fashion illustration in New York since the early 1970's has been vividly alive. Examples to prove this are: one illustrating category in which elegance is expressed using the traditional and classical technique and various techniques or touches that have been developed along with the changes in fashion sense. Take for example, Art Nouveau to Art Deco which appeared on the cover of the first issue of *Vogue*, the tendency towards surrealism from the 1930's through the 1940's, or urban and modern illustration in the 1950's. These illustrations sufficiently express their newly-born beauty of the mode. Furthermore, pop-tone and new art expressions are tending to be adopted for illustration.

In this way, all the "current" senses such as custom, atmosphere, men and women's scenes in cities at that time, are caught exactly for fashion illustration. It is created by each artist's taste or sense of beauty. This is very attractive and worthy for illustrators.

These fifteen carefully selected artists have always attracted and stimulated me for the past fifteen years while having their work appear in the *New York Times*, *Woman's Wear Daily*, *Vogue* and so on. They are extremely wonderful people.

I deeply appreciate these fifteen people who helped me compile this publication by offering their illustrations and other materials.

Pater Sato (Translation arranged by World Information Network Co., Ltd.)
December 1984

ファッション・イラストレーションというのは，流行が常に変化していくように，その表現スタイルも変わっていくのが本領だと思います。アントニオ・ロペスはいみじくも言ったものです。「自分は同じスタイルを2度とくり返さない」

この言葉がファッション・イラストレーションというもののひとつのキー・ポイントだと言えるでしょう。

僕がニューヨークのファッション・イラストレーターたちの仕事に注目し始めたのは，70年代の初め頃でした。それは自分自身の表現の方法やスタイルへの関心が，たまたまファッション・イラストレーションに向かい始めた時期でもあったのです。

時々訪れていたニューヨークでは，「ニューヨーク・タイムス」のファッション・セクションを見るのが楽しみでした。そこには各デパートのファッション広告がいっせいに掲載されるのです。ニューヨークにおけるファッション・イラストレーションの最もプレステージの高い仕事の場は，このデパートメント・ストアのイラストレーションによる広告なのです。

伝統的なトーンを好む，「ボンウィット・テーラー」や「B・アルトマン」といったデパートメント・ストアの広告は，J. クロフォードやジム・ハワードといった，50年代の頃から一貫して変らないオーソドックスなスタイル画の世界を展開するし，高級デパートといわれる「ボーグドルフ・グッドマン」は，80年代になってペンシル画のスタイルで独特の世界を切り拓いたジョージ・スタヴリノスを起用しています。また「メイシーズ」や「ブルーミングデールズ」は若い新しいアーティストを積極的に起用するなどデパートメント・ストアの広告によって，僕はニューヨークのファッション・イラストレーションの世界とその動向を知ったのでした。また日刊のファッション情報新聞「ウーマンズウェア・デイリー」を舞台に活躍するイラストレーターたちの仕事も魅力的でした。アントニオ・ロペスはここから出発していますし，現在メイシーズの広告で活躍しているジョエル・レズニコフやペドロ・バリオスといったアーティストを知ったのもこの新聞で，一方，「アメリカン・ヴォーグ」誌からはデビッド・クローランドやマッツ・グスタブソンの活躍を知りました。

70年の初めから現在に至るニューヨークのファッション・イラストレーションの流れは，オーソドックスな手法で，エレガンスを表現するといった古典的な描法が今だにひとつのジャンルとして，魅力を失わない一方では，ファッションの感覚の変遷に伴って，さまざまな手法やタッチが生みだされています。「ヴォーグ」の創刊当時のカバー・イラストレーションに見られる，アール・ヌーボー調からアール・デコへ，そして30年代から40年代にかけてみられるシュール・リアリズムへの傾倒，50年代に入ってからは都会的でモダンな傾向のイラストレーションが生み出され，新しく生まれ変わったモードの美をあますところなく伝えてくれます。さらにポップ調，最近ではニュー・アートの表現も巧みにとり入れられる傾向にあります。

こうしてファッション・イラストレーションというのは，常にその時代の匂いや風俗，都市の空気や男と女の情景に至るあらゆる“現在”の感覚が正確にとらえられ，それぞれのアーティストの美的趣向によって描き出されていくところが，僕にとっても魅力的であり，また表現する側での醍醐味でもあるのです。

ここに選んだ15名のアーティストは，いずれもこの15年間にニューヨーク・タイムスやウーマンズウェア・デイリー紙，ヴォーグ誌などで，僕を常に魅了し，また刺激し続けてくれた，すばらしい人たちです。

最後に，この本をまとめるにあたって，図版の提供など積極的に協力して頂いた，15名の彼らに心から感謝します。

ペーター佐藤
1984年12月

ペーター佐藤 Pater Sato

1945年＝神奈川県横須賀市に生まれる。東京都立日比谷高校卒業。
セツ・モードセミナーを卒業する。1977年＝ジャパニーズ・グラフィック展
'77(アメリカ)に入選。1979年＝フィンランド・ポスター・ビエンナーレに
入賞。1980年＝プレイボーイ・コレクション(アメリカ)に入選。1984年＝
コミュニケーション・アーツ誌優秀賞受賞。
著書に、《SUBJECTS》《ニューヨークの仕事場から》（PARCO出版）
がある。
アトリエ＝〒150 東京都渋谷区神宮前2-31-18　Pero 2F
ペーター・スタジオ　(03)478-1860
連絡先＝ペイジワン(03)402-8884

ファッション イラストレーション イン ニューヨーク

初版第1刷発行　1985年1月25日

編著―――――ペーター佐藤 C
発行者―――――久世利郎
印刷―――――錦明印刷株式会社
製本―――――錦明印刷株式会社
和文写植―――株式会社 プロスタディオ
欧文写植―――株式会社 タイムリー
発行―――――株式会社 グラフィック社
　　　　　　〒102　東京都千代田区九段北1-9-12
　　　　　　TEL. 東京 03-263-4318　振替 東京 3-114345
定価―――――2,500円

ISBN4-7661-0325-4 C3071 ¥2500E